P9-DDN-436

"Father Hartin's book provides an excellent entry point for those interested in exploring biblically based Christian spiritualities. Hartin begins by defining such spiritualities as rooted in the incarnation. Utilizing a productive mix of historical critical insights, Hartin demonstrates how various Gospel values were adapted in several contexts between the 2nd and 20th century. This alone would make the book a worthwhile read. But then Hartin presses on to present possiblities for those who seek to bring to life similar values as avenues of transformation in the contemporary world.

—*Kenneth G. Stenstrup, Ph.D.*
Assistant Professor of Theology
Saint Mary's University, Minnesota

"In his most recent, wonderully accessible book, Patrick Hartin offers the reader a thoughtful exploration of the spirituality of the four canonical gospels. The features that make this such an outstanding entry in the crowded field of books on 'biblical spirituality' are two in particular. Hartin's jargon free, splendidly lucid definition of Christian spirituality is in itself worth the price of the book. Adding immeasurably to the value, though, is his equally straightforward approach to reading the gospels of Jesus with the results of historical—critical analysis at hand, but not dominating his presentation, and then letting the gospels' portrait of Jesus inform his sketch of each gospel's spirituality for today. The icing on the cake is a nicely wrought closing chapter that briefly sketches the gospels' spirituality incarnate in great heroes of the faith."

—*Robert Kugler*
Paul S. Wright Professor of Christian Studies
Lewis & Clark College
Portland, Oregon

"For those readers looking for a spiritual vision that is more than pious wishes, that has real content, Patrick Hartin's book is ideal. Hartin deftly weaves together spiritual exploration with a study of the Gospels that reflects the best of historical and literary methods. He then incarnates this spirituality for his readers by lifting up lives such as Antony, Dorothy Day, Oscar Romero, and Augustine whose spiritual vision was rooted in the Gospels. Nuanced, subtle, yet very accessible, Hartin's work offers a gracious reading of the Gospels. It is ideally suited for Catholic undergraduate and church audiences, but would appeal to non-Catholic readers too."

—*Amy C. Merrill Willis*
Lynchburg College
Lynchburg, Virginia

Exploring the Spirituality of the Gospels

Patrick J. Hartin

LITURGICAL PRESS
Collegeville, Minnesota

www.litpress.org

Nihil Obstat: Reverend Robert Harren, *Censor deputatus.*

Imprimatur: ✠ Most Reverend John F. Kinney, J.C.D., D.D., Bishop of St. Cloud, Minnesota, October 18, 2010.

Cover design by Ann Blattner. Illustration: *Symbols of the Four Evangelists.* Bible of Evert von Soudenbalch, Utrecht (Northern Netherlands), c. 1460.

Scripture texts in this work are taken from the *New American Bible with Revised New Testament and Revised Psalms* © 1991, 1986, 1970 Confraternity of Christian Doctrine, Washington, DC, and are used by permission of the copyright owner. All Rights Reserved. No part of the *New American Bible* may be reproduced in any form without permission in writing from the copyright owner.

© 2011 by Order of Saint Benedict, Collegeville, Minnesota. All rights reserved. No part of this book may be reproduced in any form, by print, microfilm, microfiche, mechanical recording, photocopying, translation, or by any other means, known or yet unknown, for any purpose except brief quotations in reviews, without the previous written permission of Liturgical Press, Saint John's Abbey, PO Box 7500, Collegeville, Minnesota 56321-7500. Printed in the United States of America.

1	2	3	4	5	6	7	8	9

Library of Congress Cataloging-in-Publication Data

Hartin, P. J. (Patrick J.)
   Exploring the spirituality of the Gospels / Patrick J. Hartin.
      p. cm.
   Includes bibliographical references (p.   ) and indexes.
   ISBN 978-0-8146-3317-5 (pbk.) — ISBN 978-0-8146-3941-2 (e-book)
   1. Bible. N.T. Gospels—Criticism, interpretation, etc.   2. Spirituality—Biblical teaching.   I. Title.
   BS2555.52.H37 2011
   248—dc22   2010042946

Contents

Acknowledgments

I am indebted to all those with whom I have been privileged to engage in the study and reading of the Scriptures. One important influence on my understanding of the Scriptures has always been my students, who have challenged me in many ways and who sent me off in directions I had never imagined for my research.

I have written this book, *Exploring the Spirituality of the Gospels*, with students in mind, both college students as well as members of Bible study groups and those reading the Scriptures on their own. All who seek a deeper understanding of the spiritual vision of the Scriptures, especially the New Testament, will find insight and enrichment as it speaks to and challenges their lives.

This present study is an outgrowth of a class on the foundations of Christian spirituality that I have taught for many years. I think I have learned as much from my students as I hope they have learned from me.

In particular, I should like to mention two of those students, Bryan Zerr and James Fenske, who read and commented on my manuscript throughout the many stages of its growth. I owe an enormous gratitude to both for our many hours of conversations as they progressively read through the different chapters in their various forms. Their insights, challenges, and suggestions have resulted in a much better work as I strive to communicate my understanding of the spirituality of the gospels in ways that speak to our present world.

I also wish to express my thanks to Stephen Barbarossa for his careful construction of the index of persons and subjects found at the end of the book. Finally, I should like to thank all the editors at Liturgical Press for their assistance and guidance throughout the whole process, especially Hans Christoffersen, Stephanie Lancour, Mary Stommes, Stephanie Nix, and Colleen Stiller, as well as Cackie Upchurch, director of Little Rock Scripture Study.

I dedicate this book to Bishop Cupich (Bishop of the Diocese of Spokane) and to Bishop Skylstad (Bishop Emeritus) as well as to my confreres in the Spokane Presbyterate who have supported and encouraged me in my scholarly endeavors.

Patrick J. Hartin

Spokane

Feast of St. Augustine, August 28, 2010

Introduction

In this book, *Exploring the Spirituality of the Gospels*, I invite you, the reader, to embark on a journey through the gospels of Matthew, Mark, Luke, and John to discover their spiritual vision. As part of Sacred Scripture, these gospels provide the foundation for the faith and life of Christians. Our exploration takes seriously Scripture as Scripture. Composed by people inspired by God's Spirit, Scripture communicates God's word through human words. The meaning of what the human authors had to say is the focus of our journey as well as the understanding that Scripture continues to speak God's message to the lives of every generation and, in particular, to people today.

Our journey of exploration through these four early witnesses to the person and vision of Jesus seeks to discover the important themes, values, and ideas that have become foundational for spiritual traditions over the course of the centuries and that continue to speak to our present world. We view this "speaking to our world" in two ways: giving attention to aspects that resonate within our world, and taking seriously those dimensions that also challenge our world. Resonance and challenge work together in transforming the lives of believers. The spiritual message of Christianity is a message both formative and transformative: it forms believers in the vision opened up by the writings of Scripture; it transforms by illuminating ways believers can be changed into the image of Christ.

This book is a study in *biblical spirituality*. Spirituality is an area of thought that excites people of every walk of life today, as chapter 1 will show. The term spirituality has a long and varied history within Christianity. However, in seventeenth-century France there was an awakening of interest in spirituality understood as the Christian's journey through sanctification in the spiritual life.[1] While much has been written today on different trends and traditions within Christianity, in this book I invite you, the reader, behind these traditions to explore the roots of spirituality in the foundational documents of Christianity, the gospels. Whatever calls itself *Christian spirituality* must be based on their foundation and must always return to them to renew and revive its spiritual energy. Hopefully, this study will deepen and open for you the depth and breadth of the spiritual vision of the gospels.

A word needs to be said about the *methodology* used in this book. In the context of the Catholic Church, the historical-critical method has been endorsed as basic for any study of the Scriptures.[2] The Christian faith speaks about real events that occurred in history. To understand the Christian faith one must understand the foundation on which it stands. Such an understanding can only be approached by using the historical and critical tools necessary to interpret it.[3]

But, methods of interpretation must always be attuned to the purpose for which they are used. By its very nature, the historical-critical method aims at interpreting the past. It is interested in the history, origin, and growth of the text. As part of Sacred Scripture, the gospels are not simply documents from two thousand years ago. They also have significance and meaning for the lives of those who read them. In order to explore the spiritual dimensions of the gospels, we need to build on and go beyond the historical-critical method. As part of Sacred Scripture, the gospels belong to that theological and religious message of God's communication with humanity through the person of Jesus. They were ultimately recorded and transmitted for the faith of future generations. This present exploration discovers how the gospels relate the experience of the person of God in Jesus and how this experience transforms readers.

The approach adopted in exploring the spirituality of each of the gospels unfolds in two parts. The first part forms the center of our exploration, namely, the discovery of the spiritual vision of each gospel. The second part will offer brief illustrations of the distinctive transformative power of that spirituality in the lives of people who embraced that vision.

Part One: Exploring the Spiritual Vision of the Gospels
(Chapters Two through Five)

The spiritual vision of each gospel emerges from an examination of two questions:

Who is Jesus? Each gospel writer reflects on the person of Jesus to present a distinctive understanding of Jesus.

What transformative response does this encounter with Jesus invite? In reflecting on the experience of Jesus' early followers, each writer draws out the responses that believers are called to emulate.

Part Two: Biblical Spirituality: Incarnate and Alive (Chapter Six)

Examples will be given to illustrate those Christians who modeled their lives and thought on the spiritual vision of these gospels. These brief explorations will indicate the distinctive way in which they appropriated in their lives aspects of the gospel's spiritual vision. The following remarkable Christians will be considered:

From the past: St. Antony, Sts. Perpetua and Felicity, St. Francis of Assisi, and St. Augustine.

From more recent times: Dorothy Day, Archbishop Romero, St. Damien of Molokai, and St. Teresa Benedicta of the Cross (Edith Stein).

Throughout our exploration of the different spiritual visions of the gospels and the lives of those who incarnated their spirituality, we will indicate their relevance and importance for readers today. My hope is that this exploration will animate and challenge you, the reader, along your journey of transformation according to the image of Christ.

CHAPTER ONE

Context for Exploring Biblical Spirituality

In recent years, interest in the area of spirituality has proliferated. Our culture exhibits a lively awareness that the human person is more than a physical body. In a recent visit to a local bookstore, I discovered under a section classified as "spirituality" items such as the following: New Age spirituality, spirituality of relationships, tarot cards. Surprisingly, there was no indication that Christianity had anything to do with spirituality since no works on Christian spirituality were filed there! A simple search on the web under the word "spirituality" produced some sixty-one million hits! These sites embraced everything from astrology to Zen and included mediums and psychic reading guides, shamanism and spiritism, New Age and kabbalah inspired spirituality. Christian spirituality was lost among this plethora of offerings.

The above trends illustrate how our culture seeks to satisfy a spiritual thirst at the beginning of the twenty-first century. The twelve-step program, developed by Alcoholics Anonymous, for example, is an important spiritual process that continues to offer support and guidance to millions of people struggling to overcome alcohol addiction. The spiritual dimensions emerge clearly from the steps that include the recognition that one has a serious problem, the acknowledgment that an outside Power could help, and turning to that Power through prayer and meditation to overcome the problem. This program has been successfully adapted by numerous other groups also facing similar life-debilitating and -dependent issues, such as Narcotics Anonymous,

Overeaters Anonymous, and Codependents Anonymous. One can also include here the numerous "self-help" books and web sites that seek to provide techniques by which people can animate their lives to overcome and deal with problematic issues.

Without doubt, this new phenomenon within our culture shows a need to satisfy a spiritual hunger that is evident almost everywhere. In a materialist society with such a wealth of goods, opportunities, possessions, the human person still feels unsatisfied, still longs for something more. This "something more" can only be satisfied by devoting attention to an essential dimension of the human person: the spirit or the soul. These works on spirituality aim at answering this spiritual hunger at the core of the human person.

Toward a Definition of Spirituality

In its most basic sense, *spiritual* is defined as "pertaining to the spirit or soul, as distinguished from the physical nature."[1] The spirit is contrasted to the body, the material dimension of the human person. The spirit identifies that which gives life, that which animates. In the biblical writings, *spirit* (Latin, *spiritus*; Greek, *pneuma*; Hebrew, *ruah*) denotes "the human spirit, the breath of life," which is not simply part of a human person, but rather the whole being.

The spirit is also used in a deeper sense in the biblical writings. Since God is Spirit, the communication of God's grace is the gift of God's life to us. Our spirits are imbued with God's Spirit. When Paul extends his greetings in his letters and says, "The grace of our Lord Jesus Christ be with your spirit, brothers [and sisters]" (Gal 6:18), he is referring to the communication of God's gift of life to their whole being. Likewise, when Jesus speaks to Nicodemus in John's gospel, he also refers to the communication of God's Spirit to the human spirit: "What is born of flesh is flesh and what is born of spirit is spirit. . . . The wind blows where it wills, and you can hear the sound it makes, but you do not know where it comes from or where it goes; so it is with everyone who is born of the Spirit" (John 3:6, 8).

Originally, the term spirituality was used in a religious and Christian context to refer to the mystical encounter between the individual and God that was expressed in a devotional life of prayer and pious practices. Today, the understanding of spirituality has broadened to such an extent that in popular culture spirituality and religion appear to be separated from each other. Often I hear students say, "I have a deep spirituality, but I am not particularly religious." In this sense, religion refers to any organized, structured, traditional religion, whereas spirituality embraces the freedom of the human spirit to encounter the divine in surprisingly unexpected ways. Formerly, spirituality lay at the heart of religion and gave expression to its essence by a way of life. Today, in popular imagination, spirituality is divorced from religion. The spiritual hunger evident in our culture is satisfied in ways independent of any formalized religion. Another search on the internet revealed that the phrase "spirituality versus religion" resulted in an astonishing 165 million sites (almost three times more than spirituality on its own)!

Dissatisfaction is expressed with religious institutions because they appear to stifle and bind the human spirit in its quest for an authentic experience of the sacred or the divine. Religion is identified with rules, regulations, customs that are presented as suffocating and life-annihilating. For this reason, appeal is made to a spirituality that rests upon the subjective experience and severs every connection with religion.

Yet, religion need not be viewed in such a narrow, negative, and restrictive sense. Surely, religion's main purpose is to communicate an experience of the divine, of the sacred. Religion accomplishes this in many ways: through rituals, prayers, and devotional practices. One important way of fostering an encounter with the divine is through the reading of its sacred texts. These writings transmit the foundational experiences of the sacred within that religion for people of every generation who wish to make their own this spiritual heritage. One learns from others, one stands on the shoulders of others, one is supported by others who have a similar quest for the ultimate integration of all that gives meaning to life.

Given the breadth of the usage of the term "spirituality" today, it is important to provide a definition that would embrace those aspects essential to the human experience that are currently classified as "spirituality." Sandra Schneiders has offered a very helpful definition of spirituality. She presents an understanding of spirituality that is open to the vast array of trends identified today under this umbrella. Schneiders defines spirituality in this way:

> In short, spirituality refers to the experience of consciously striving to integrate one's life in terms not of isolation and self-absorption but of self-transcendence toward the ultimate value one perceives.[2]

Schneiders sees spirituality encompassing whatever gives life ultimate meaning and direction. Spirituality provides the impulse that drives a person's actions and integrates within the human person those ultimate values that provide meaning. This search for integration is vital in the culture of the twenty-first century where the world and the individual within this culture appear so widely fragmented. Based upon the above, I offer the following definition of spirituality:

> ### Spirituality
>
> *The search to integrate life*
> *through whatever animates and*
> *provides ultimate meaning and direction*

✓ Christian Spirituality

Christian spirituality is defined by the adjective *Christian*. The pulsating heart of Christian spirituality is Jesus Christ. The message and person of Christ animates the existence of Christians and gives them meaning and direction through the power of the Spirit. Central to the concept of Christian spirituality is its community dimension. Believers are united together in a common search for the sacred that is encountered through the person of Jesus Christ. Christians from former generations and centuries continue to bear witness to the way in which they encountered and appropriated the person of Christ as made known in the Scriptures. As the Letter to the Hebrews says, "we are surrounded by so great a cloud of witnesses . . ." (12:1). A whole tradition has developed over the course of the centuries beginning with those first witnesses to the experience of Jesus Christ as reflected in the Christian Scriptures.

Gustavo Gutierrez, in his work *We Drink from Our Own Wells: The Spiritual Journey of a People*,[3] offers a reflection on the development of a Christian spiritual tradition. The three stages that he identifies are extremely significant for understanding biblical spirituality:

> *The Experience of Encounter:* In every spiritual tradition there is an initial starting point where an encounter with the Lord occurs. This encounter is a privileged moment giving meaning and direction to the lives of those experiencing it. In the pages of the gospels, we have testimony to these encounters in the lives of Jesus' early disciples. When they first encountered Jesus, he challenged them to follow

him (Mark 1:17). Saul of Tarsus is another example. By encountering the risen Lord, his life was transformed: "'Saul, Saul, why are you persecuting me?' He said, 'Who are you, sir?'" (Acts 9:4-5). The life of the writer of the book of Revelation also experienced God's transforming power: "I was caught up in spirit on the Lord's day and heard behind me a voice as loud as a trumpet" (Rev 1:10).

Reflection: This spiritual experience leads to a deeper reflection on its meaning and importance. Over the course of many decades, Jesus' followers try to make sense of their experiences. In subsequent ages of the Christian church, the same reflection on experience continues. In the fourth century, St. Augustine experienced a spiritual encounter with the Lord and reflected upon this experience further in his *Confessions.* As Gutierrez says, "To reflect theologically on a spiritual experience means to work through it by relating it to the word of the Lord, to thinking of one's own age, and to other ways of understanding the following of Jesus."[4]

Prolongation: Reflection on this spiritual experience of encounter is ultimately placed in writing for the purpose of sharing this way of living with the community of believers. After many decades of reflection on the message and person of Jesus, the gospel writers committed to writing their insights and reflections for their respective communities. Consequently, within the New Testament different spiritualities emerged, providing diverse ways of living in response to the encounter with the Lord. Over the course of future centuries, other Christians also endeavored to record their own spiritual journeys that were in their turn marked by an encounter with Jesus Christ and a deep reflection on this life-changing experience.

The above discussion shows that the *Christian* dimension of spirituality embraces an *experience of encounter* with the person of Jesus the Christ, which leads to a *reflection* upon this experience and its significance in the context of the totality of life.

From this brief analysis, we offer the following definition of Christian spirituality:

Christian Spirituality

The search to integrate life
through the transforming experience of
encountering God in Christ.
This experience animates and gives life
meaning and direction.

Biblical Spirituality

Jesus' early followers communicated their insights and experiences in writing in the Sacred Scriptures that provide the foundation for the Christian faith. Since these Scriptures express the fullness of God's revelation in God's Son, Jesus Christ, they are normative for the Christian way of life. As a tree needs roots to grow, to draw nourishment and be sustained, so Christian spirituality needs to be rooted in the Scriptures for its own growth, nourishment, and sustenance.

The gospels are documents of faith. Each evangelist is intent on transmitting his experience, his reflection, and the transforming power of the presence of God encountered in Jesus. Each evangelist also wishes to evoke a response from the reader. From this intended purpose in writing, two poles emerge in this study of biblical spirituality, namely, reflection upon God encountered in the person of Jesus and the response believers are called to give through their actions and the type of life they lead. Each biblical writer embraces and communicates to his readers his own overarching *vision* of Jesus and challenges every believer to embrace this way of life. By *vision*, I understand the unifying perspective or picture the biblical writer envisages regarding Jesus and its implications for the life of believers. A brief overview of each of the gospels will show their respective visions:

The Gospel of Matthew has its vision emerge from reflecting on the gospel's beginning ("'. . . and they shall name him Emmanuel,' which means, 'God is with us'" [Matt 1:23]) and ending ("And behold, I am with you always, until the end of the age" [Matt 28:20]). Matthew's vision centers on Jesus as "God with us." This belief continues to hold true for readers at all times. Matthew wishes to show what transformation that experience of Jesus as "God with us" should have for his readers. Just as

God was continually present among his people, Israel, so Jesus continues his presence among the new people of God. In the past, God's presence demanded of his people: "Be holy, for I, the LORD your God, am holy" (Lev 19:2). Now among the new people of God their lives are challenged anew: "So be perfect, just as your heavenly Father is perfect" (Matt 5:48).

The Gospel of Mark emerges from a reflection on the experience of Jesus' suffering and death as well as the experiences of many of Jesus' first followers sentenced to a fate similar to their master. Mark's vision pictures Jesus as the suffering Messiah of God who gave his life "as a ransom for many" (Mark 10:45). This vision of the person of Jesus leads Mark to challenge his readers to do likewise, to embrace the experience of suffering and death they were currently encountering in the spirit of Jesus. In response to James and John, who request the privilege of sharing his power when he enters into his kingdom, Jesus foretells that they will indeed share in his suffering: "'Can you drink the cup that I drink or be baptized with the baptism with which I am baptized?' They said to him, 'We can.' Jesus said to them, 'The cup that I drink, you will drink, and with the baptism with which I am baptized, you will be baptized'" (Mark 10:38-39).

The Gospel of Luke, from the hand of a third-generation Christian, looks back on the person of Jesus (Luke 1:1-4). He views the life and ministry of Jesus from the perspective of one who has experienced the message of Jesus spread beyond the borders of Jerusalem "to the ends of the earth" (Acts 1:8). For the writer of the Gospel of Luke, the Acts of the Apostles is essential to continue his reflection on Jesus and his message by focusing on the experiences of Jesus' followers who handed on his message after he had returned to the Father. Luke's vision emerges from this background. Jesus is the Savior of the world and this universal salvation is concretely illustrated throughout the gospel narrative in Jesus' outreach to the poor and those marginalized in any way by society. The readers are challenged to embrace that same outreach as exemplified in the lives of Jesus' early followers, such as Peter, and Paul. Every generation is meant to embrace this vision expressed so clearly in the words that Jesus addressed to his first followers: "But you will receive power when the holy Spirit comes upon you, and you will be my witnesses . . . to the ends of the earth" (Acts 1:8).

The Gospel of John is the result of sixty years of in-depth reflection on the experience and significance of Jesus. Because of its meditative nature, Clement of Alexandria, in the second century AD, referred to it as the "Spiritual Gospel." The vision of the Gospel of John rests on the firm belief that Jesus is the Word who became flesh and lived among us to enable us to become "children of God." The Word bears witness to the Father. Through the person of Jesus, the glory of the Father emerges: "'Have I been with you for so long a time and you still do not know me, Philip? Whoever has seen me has seen the Father'" (John 14:9). The consequences for the reader become immediately evident at the conclusion to the gospel itself: "But these are written so that you may [come to] believe that Jesus is the Messiah, the Son of God, and that through this belief you may have life in his name" (John 20:31). Readers are invited to experience this transformation through their belief in Jesus: "But to those who did accept him he gave power to become children of God, to those who believe in his name, who were born not by natural generation nor by human choice nor by a man's decision but of God" (John 1:12-13).

As indicated above, each gospel's vision embraces two central aspects, the experience of God in the person of Jesus and the response this experience invites from his followers. The spiritual vision of each gospel will be explored more fully in the chapters that follow.

Biblical Spirituality

The search for believers to integrate life
through the spiritual vision of those biblical writings
that witness to an encounter with God in the person of Jesus
and the response required by their transformed life.

Appropriating the Spirituality of the Gospels within the Context of Communities of Faith

Our study explores the spiritual vision of each gospel. In doing so, we need to keep in mind two contexts. The first context is the understanding of the spiritual vision that emerges from these writings within the world of Jesus and of the gospel writers themselves. The second context is that of later readers who look to the foundational dimension of the Scriptures in order to appropriate its spiritual vision within a world far different from the originating documents.

In exploring the spiritual vision of the gospels, attention will be given to reading the gospels responsibly. As indicated in the introduction, the historical-critical method is presumed in this investigation. However, the aim is far broader than simply understanding texts from the past. We wish to explore how the spiritual vision of the person of Jesus with its values and ideals transforms the way of life of his followers. To understand this vision, the individual writings must be read in the context of the unity of Scripture[5] where the earlier writings point to the future, and the future writings give deeper meaning to those of the past. As part of Sacred Scripture, the gospels belong to that theological and religious message of God's communication with humanity through the person of Jesus recorded and transmitted for the faith of future generations.

This inquiry into the relevance and meaning of the text of Scripture for today's reader raises the question, what exactly is appropriated today when one reads the gospels? The philosopher Paul Ricoeur defines appropriation in this way:

> *What has to be appropriated is the meaning of the text itself, conceived in a dynamic way as the direction of thought opened up by the text.* In other words, what has to be appropriated is nothing other than the power of disclosing a world that constitutes the reference of the text.[6]

These words express exactly what we have referred to in this chapter as "the vision" that the biblical writer is expressing within the context of his historical and cultural world. In exploring the spirituality of the gospels, the focus will be on this central aspect, the meaning of the text that is opened up, or the *spiritual vision* that the biblical writer communicates. Then, in part 2 (chap. 6) we will illustrate how this spiritual vision has been appropriated at different ages of the church's history and continues to be appropriated in our world today.

In appropriating this spiritual vision of the Scriptures within the framework of the modern world, the gospel must be encountered in a way that speaks to each individual's inner self and gives meaning and direction. The individual journey of faith must be respected. This individual journey, however, is not undertaken in isolation from others but occurs within the context of a faith community where the individual forges connections and bonds. In 2007, Archbishop Wilson, president of the Australian Catholic Bishops' Conference, expressed well this interconnectedness between the individual journey and the community of faith:

In an expressivist age,[7] believers must recognize the individual quest of every person and lead each one to discover the Gospel as God's clearest word about their lives and the community of Jesus' disciples as the place where his life is made most manifest in the world today. Forcing religious belief makes no sense in this culture. The faith community must lead others to the discovery that the Gospel makes sense of their being.[8]

While it is important to have an insightful understanding of the present culture, the gospel's vision is meant to be transformative of this culture. The challenge is to present the spiritual vision of each gospel so that it is seen as the foundational truth that gives meaning to the spiritual journey. In exploring the spiritual vision of each gospel, this study will open up that spiritual vision for the reader, as an individual and as part of a community of faith, to discover anew the person of Jesus and the response that spiritual vision demands. This encounter should enable individuals to appropriate this spiritual vision for their inner selves and give direction and meaning to their lives. Then, in part 2 (chap. 6), through the lives of individual men and women within the community of Christians over the centuries, we will show how this vision continues to be appropriated.

PART ONE

Exploring the Spiritual Vision of the Gospels:
Matthew, Mark, Luke, and John

(Chapters Two through Five)

CHAPTER TWO

Exploring Matthew's Spiritual Vision

As the most popular of the gospels in the early church, the Gospel of Matthew was placed first in the New Testament canon. Matthew's gospel has deeply influenced the thought and spirituality of the Christian church. The liturgy of the Catholic Church embraced Matthew's version of so many New Testament passages, such as the form of the Our Father. The significance of Matthew's Sermon on the Mount is also unique for its presentation of the spiritual life that Christians and non-Christians alike see as the finest expression of the heart of Christianity.

From a close study of the Gospel of Matthew, scholars agree that this gospel was written at a time of definition and struggle for identity. The forceful opposition in the gospel between Jesus and the Jewish authorities, especially the Pharisees, shows a struggle for the heart and soul of the spiritual traditions of the people of Israel. Following the destruction of the temple of Jerusalem in AD 70, the nature of the worship of Israel changed from one centered on sacrificial offerings in the temple to one inspired by the Torah (the Law) that aimed at the sanctification of daily life. Two Jewish groups survived the temple's destruction, namely, the Pharisees and the followers of Jesus. The Pharisees replaced the temple with the Torah that guided daily life. Jesus' followers, on the other hand, centered their way of life on the person of Jesus, his message and example. Each group claimed to be the true heir to Israel's traditions. This explains the harshness of the description of the Pharisees in Matthew's gospel: "Woe to you, scribes and Pharisees, you hypocrites. You are like whitewashed tombs . . ." (23:27).

13

Against this backdrop of opposition and conflict, the Gospel of Matthew emerged in the mid-eighties of the Christian era, some five decades after the death and resurrection of Jesus. Matthew[1] decided to write a gospel for his own community situated in Antioch of Syria. A large number of Jesus' followers were living there (as both the letter of Paul to the Galatians and the Acts of the Apostles testify). Studies on the relationship among the gospels have shown that Mark was the first to write a gospel and that Matthew used Mark's gospel as its foundation. In addition to Mark's gospel, Matthew used another source, the Sayings Source Q,[2] a compendium of Jesus' sayings. From these Q sayings, Matthew compiled five major sermons. In addition, Matthew also had access to some further material. From three sources, Mark (as the foundation), the Sayings of Q, and his own material, Matthew composed a gospel to speak to the issues and concerns of his community in Antioch. In producing his gospel, Matthew offered a spiritual vision of the person of Jesus and the challenge that vision presented for the life of his community. In doing so, Matthew showed how Jesus' vision remained true to the heart and heritage of Israel's traditions.

The essence of the dispute with the Pharisees concerned faithful adherence to Israel's traditions and heritage. The focus of Matthew's gospel lay with Jesus' teachings and his interpretation of the Torah. For the people of Israel, the Torah meant "law, teaching, instruction." Specifically, the Torah referred to the first five books of the Bible that contained God's instructions, teachings, laws for the way God's people were to live their lives in fidelity to God's covenant. The heart of Jesus' approach to interpreting Israel's Torah is summed up by his words, "Do not think that I have come to abolish the law or the prophets. I have come not to abolish but to fulfill" (5:17). Matthew's gospel intended to remind his hearers that Jesus taught a fuller understanding of the meaning and interpretation of God's will for the people of his own time and for Matthew's community living in a new age.

Encountering God in the Person of Jesus

The Road of the Past Leads to Jesus

The Gospel of Matthew acts like a hinge holding together the Old and New Testaments. Fundamental to Matthew's spiritual vision is Jesus' relationship to Israel's heritage. Matthew's gospel gives direct attention to this connection in its two opening chapters that contain material specific to the gospel itself. On five occasions Matthew quotes from the Old Testament, saying unambiguously, "All this took place to fulfill what the Lord had said through the prophet" (1:22-23; 2:5-6; 2:15; 2:17-18; 2:23).

The gospel opens by proclaiming forthrightly that Jesus Christ is "the son of David, the son of Abraham" (1:1). The rest of the gospel illustrates this claim. The gospel's opening paragraph (1:1-17) deliberately forges Jesus' connection to Israel's heritage by means of a *genealogy*, a list that traces Jesus' ancestry back in time to Abraham. A cursory glance at the Old Testament writings shows how important the people of Israel considered it to identify the ancestry of each of their significant figures. A genealogy gave the person an identity within the context of the history of their nation. This is strikingly similar to the fascination people have today for discovering their own background and heritage.

At first sight, this list of unfamiliar names (1:1-17) appears somewhat disconcerting and unintelligible. However, a closer look at this genealogy reveals a direction and context for Matthew's spiritual vision. Three important aspects emerge for the spirituality of Matthew's gospel:

- *"The book of the genealogy of Jesus Christ, the son of David, the son of Abraham"* (1:1).[3] These opening words immediately remind the reader of the first book of the Old Testament. The Septuagint, the Greek translation of the Old Testament, gave this book the title "Genesis" (from the Greek *genesis*), referring to an account of someone's origin, life, or history.[4] Matthew used this same word to identify his writing as "the book of the [*genesis*] of Jesus Christ . . ." (1:1). Just as the first book of the Bible contained an account of the origin of God's creation, so Matthew's gospel contains an account of the origin of Jesus Christ. Matthew draws attention to God's spiritual vision that God is beginning a new creation with the birth of Jesus. Matthew's intention is to witness to this new creation and draw out its implications for the believer.

- *God had this spiritual vision in mind from the beginning in creating the nation of Israel.* Matthew constructs his genealogy in such a way that it illustrates clearly God's spiritual vision. *Beginning with Abraham (the founding father of the nation), Matthew structures the history of the people of Israel into three time periods of fourteen generations each* (1:17). What is significant in structuring the genealogy around the number fourteen? To perform mathematical calculations, the Hebrews used the letters of their alphabet to represent numbers. If the letters in the name of David are given their numerical value, the name "David" adds up to fourteen (D+V+D = 4+6+4 = 14). Since King David is at the center of Israel's relationship with their God, this genealogy reflects this centrality by focusing on his name. Not only was David the historical king who created the nation of Israel with its geographical boundaries and its capital, but he was also a symbol for the people's future hopes that God would reestablish God's kingdom through a king like David. The genealogy captures this spiritual vision that the history of God's people is under God's rule and is leading to the establishment of God's kingdom with the coming Messiah. The birth of Jesus Christ, the son of David, the son of Abraham, fulfills these hopes and promises. Jesus is the long-awaited Messiah.

• In a surprising way, *reference is made in the genealogy to four women in an otherwise male dominated list of names*: "Judah became the father of Perez and Zerah, whose *mother was Tamar*" (1:3); "Boaz, whose *mother was Rahab*" (1:5); "Boaz became the father of Obed, whose *mother was Ruth*" (1:5); "David became the father of Solomon, whose *mother had been the wife of Uriah*" (1:6). In each of these four instances, the women are from outside the people of Israel. By drawing attention to them, Matthew shows God's plan working in surprising and unexpected ways. Although the genealogy lists Joseph as Mary's husband (1:16), the surprising element of Jesus' birth (1:18-25) is that "it is through the holy Spirit that this child has been conceived in her" (1:20). Surprisingly as well, God's plan embraces not only the people of Israel but *also the Gentile world*. This prepares the way for the spiritual message at the end of the gospel that Jesus' message is to be proclaimed to the Gentile world (28:18-20).

Jesus Is "God with Us"

Jesus is presented in this gospel as son of David, son of Abraham (1:1), Messiah (1:16), Lord (8:2, 6, 8), and Teacher (Rabbi [19:16]). The foundational image that controls Jesus' unfolding ministry and teaching is that he is "God with us." This belief that God's presence is in Jesus emerges at the very beginning of the narrative. Matthew narrates the birth of Jesus and then adds a quotation from the prophet Isaiah: "All this took place to fulfill what the Lord had said through the prophet: 'Behold, the virgin shall be with child and bear a son, and they shall name him Emmanuel,' which means 'God is with us'" (1:22-23). God's presence is at work in the very birth of Jesus "from a virgin." Jesus is God's presence among us human beings.

This spiritual vision of God's presence in Jesus continues to unfold throughout the narrative. At his baptism (3:13-17), the Spirit of God descends upon him and a voice proclaims, "This is my beloved Son, with whom I am well pleased" (3:17). This implies that Jesus' teachings and all his actions are those of God's presence among us. The people of Israel believed that God's presence accompanied them on their wanderings through the desert in the form of a cloud by day and a pillar of fire at night (Exod 13:21-22). With the building of the temple, the people of Israel continued to believe that God was present in a special way in the temple itself. But, now in the person of Jesus, God's presence was unique: "I say to you, something greater than the temple is here" (12:6).

Matthew's spirituality rests firmly on the belief that God's presence is encountered in the person of Jesus in a way never before experienced. Matthew's description of the people's reaction to Jesus goes beyond anything that Mark's gospel had presented. People "doing homage to" Jesus occurs on at least eight different occasions (2:11; 8:2; 9:18; 14:33; 15:25; 20:20; 28:9, 17). On each of these occasions the Greek word is *proskyneō*, a term that is "frequently used to designate the custom of prostrating oneself before persons and kissing their feet or the hem of their garment, the ground, etc.; the Persians did this in the presence of their deified king, and the Greeks before a divinity or something holy."[5] When performed before human beings, this action acknowledges that they belong to the divine world. In this way, Jesus is regarded as the one in whom God's presence is evident. When Jesus rebukes the devil at the conclusion to his temptations, he says, "The Lord, your God, shall you worship [*proskyneō*] and him alone shall you serve" (4:10). Ultimately, Matthew's spirituality rests on the belief that God is present in Jesus in such a unique way that worshiping him is a worship of God himself.[6]

For Matthew, God's presence in Jesus continues among those who are baptized in his name. The risen Jesus promises his disciples before his ascension: "And, behold, I am with you always, until the end of the age" (28:20). In Jesus, God's presence with us continues forever. Elsewhere, Jesus reiterates this concept of his abiding presence. At the heart of the narrative, Jesus proclaims, "For where two or three are gathered together in my name, there am I in the midst of them" (18:20). In Jesus' final parable on the Judgment of the Nations, he proclaims, "Whatever you did for one of these least brothers of mine, you did for me" (25:40). God's abiding presence in Jesus lies at the heart of Matthew's spirituality. This presence was experienced by those who encountered Jesus during his earthly ministry and continues among God's people until the end of time. Just as Jesus' presence among his disciples transformed them, so Jesus' presence among his future followers continues to transform their lives.

Jesus Reveals God as Father

The image of God as Father lies at the heart of Matthew's spirituality and defines Jesus' own relationship with God. As God's Son, Jesus refers to his relationship in unambiguous terms when he addresses God as Father in his prayer of praise: "I give praise to you, Father, Lord of heaven and earth, for although you have hidden these things from the wise and the learned you have revealed them to the childlike" (11:25-26).

In instructing his followers how to pray (6:9-13), Jesus invites them to acknowledge their spiritual relationship with God by addressing God as Father in the same manner that Jesus does: "Our Father, in heaven . . ." Believers can call on God as Father because, as Son, Jesus has introduced them into this relationship. While Jesus prays simply "Father" or "My Father" (26:42), believers need to identify themselves with Jesus in calling on God. Their spiritual relationship with Jesus makes it possible for them to call God, Father. At the same time, they also acknowledge their relationship to one another. "Our Father" solidifies believers in their spiritual relationship with one another and with the person of Jesus.

By adding the phrase "in heaven," Matthew's Jesus reminds his hearers that while there may be similarities between our human fathers and God, nevertheless there is a major difference. This spiritual relationship is not a relationship of equals, but a relationship with God, who is totally other, who is transcendent. The following petitions define more fully this spiritual relationship between God as Father and believers. The first three petitions pray to the Father that he will be acknowledged, that the rule of his kingdom will come, that his will be embraced everywhere. The second set of petitions turns to the needs of believers who pray for God's continual care, sustenance, forgiveness, and protection from evil in their daily lives.

Spiritual Response to Jesus as God's Presence with Us

As God's presence with believers, Jesus' task is to lead them to a deeper understanding and experience of God. One way Matthew's gospel shows this is through the presentation of God as Father and Jesus as Teacher (Rabbi), who fulfills all Israel's hopes. This image of Jesus as Rabbi is reinforced through the way the gospel is structured. Five sermons form the very heart of Matthew's gospel (the Sermon on the Mount [5:1–7:27], the mission sermon [10:1-42], the parable sermon [13:1-52], the sermon on the church [18:1-35], and the eschatological sermon [24:1–25:46]). Matthew deliberately selected *five* sermons to present the essence of Jesus' teaching. For the people of Israel, the first *five* books (or the Torah) contained a record of God's will for his people by showing them how to lead their lives. In an analogous way, Matthew presents Jesus' teaching in *five sermons* for his followers. These five sermons contain the foundational direction and essential spiritual wisdom for the new people of God, showing them how they are to lead their lives. In a masterful way, these five sermons relate Jesus' teaching to that of the past, while at the same time giving it a new direction into the future.

Our exploration of the spirituality of the Gospel of Matthew centers on two of the sermons: the spiritual wisdom of the Sermon on the Mount (5:1–7:27) and the spiritual vision in Matthew's final parable on the Judgment of the Nations (25:31-46).

Sermon on the Mount (5:1–7:27)

This sermon contains the clearest expression of Jesus' spiritual vision for his followers: a design for the spiritual life of those who belong to God's kingdom. Most of Matthew's spiritual themes are expressed here for the first time. Attention will be given to the major spiritual themes that capture the essence of Matthew's spirituality.

Jesus the Authoritative Rabbi

The sermon opens with a reference to Jesus going up the mountain (5:1). The hearer/reader is reminded of Moses ascending the mountain of Sinai to receive the Ten Commandments (Exod 19:1–20:26). Jesus appears as the new Moses teaching a new law on a new Mount Sinai. By describing Jesus as sitting down, Matthew reflects the way a sermon was delivered in the context of the synagogue. This image clearly portrays Jesus as a Rabbi who teaches with authority.

Spirituality of the Beatitudes (5:2-12)

The opening address of the sermon contains nine sayings (5:2-12), called "Beatitudes" from the Latin word *beati*, meaning "blessed." These sayings promise a life of blessedness (happiness) through the gift of God's grace for those striving to lead their lives according to this vision. The Beatitudes offer a wonderful testimony to a future where there will be a reversal of fortunes. In these Beatitudes, Jesus sketches the life of a believer living under God's rule. Those who embrace these Beatitudes experience in this present time the blessings and grace of God's rule. These values are contrary to the typical values found in the Greco-Roman world and proclaim a spiritual revolution that is still in the process of unfolding.

- *"Blessed are the poor in spirit"* (5:3). The poverty of which Jesus speaks is a poverty of spirit. As a poor person depends on someone else for survival, so the follower of Jesus knows the need to depend upon God for his or her welfare. This spiritual poverty expresses the true meaning of "humility," the acknowledgment of a spiritual relationship of dependence on God. The phrase "kingdom of heaven" (at the end of verses 3 and 10) is Matthew's way of saying "kingdom of God." This expression reveals the concern the people of Israel had for avoiding even the use of the word "God" out of respect for God's name. The "kingdom of heaven" is an image that refers to God's rule over us and over our world. The spiritual relationship with God as Father that the believer is called to accept is in effect an acceptance of God's rule in one's life.

- *"Blessed are those who mourn"* (5:4). As with all the Beatitudes, this blessing is spiritualized. The mourning expresses abhorrence for the effects of sin and evil. The consolation will be to experience the salvation that has been brought by Jesus, the Messiah.

- *"Blessed are the meek"* (5:5). The "meek" embrace again the spiritual attitude of humility that expresses itself in kindness. They are promised the inheritance of a new world.

- *"Blessed are they who hunger and thirst for righteousness"* (5:6). The image of experiencing hunger and thirst is again spiritualized. A blessing is promised on those who have a deep spiritual desire to act morally in a way that carries out God's will. In the Gospel of Matthew "righteousness" refers to moral action that conforms to God's will.

- *"Blessed are the merciful"* (5:7). A blessing is promised to those who show mercy or compassion to others. Their reward is to have compassion shown them. Elsewhere Matthew's gospel speaks of the importance of mercy over sacrifice (9:13; 12:7).

- *"Blessed are the clean of heart" (5:8).* This blessing designates those who have right or good intentions and desires. Their reward is to experience God's presence.

- *"Blessed are the peacemakers" (5:9).* Blessings are promised to those who take concrete steps to restore relationships among people. This call to be "peacemakers" is further illustrated in the sermon through Jesus' teaching on loving one's enemies (5:44-48). The reward is to be called God's children.

- *"Blessed are they who are persecuted for the sake of righteousness" (5:10).* The persecution refers to what is endured in order to maintain right relations with God and carry out God's will. The reward is again to experience God's rule by entering into a spiritual relationship with God.

- *"Blessed are you when they insult you and persecute you" (5:11-12).* In this final beatitude, Jesus addresses his disciples directly. The community of disciples will experience defamation and persecution. Their joy is to be part of the "kingdom of heaven."

Throughout these Beatitudes, Jesus proclaims a spiritual way of life that begins with the acknowledgment of God's rule over the believer and over the community. God's rule begins now, only to reach its fulfillment in the future. In like manner, many of the promises made throughout these Beatitudes are experienced in a small way in the present, but the blessings will be realized in their fullness in the future.

Spiritual Wisdom of the Law (5:17-47)

The full meaning of the law is found in Jesus, who spells out very clearly his relationship to the Old Testament and its commandments (5:17-20). Jesus states that he has come not "to abolish the law or the prophets. I have come not to abolish but to fulfill" (5:17). Jesus is Lord of the law (not its servant). The law has been leading to him and he in turn is able to give the law its true meaning and understanding. In Jesus, God's will reaches its fulfillment and its full spiritual meaning is expressed.

Jesus has come not to do away with Israel's past. Instead, he has come to give the law its fullest understanding. The *antitheses* (5:21-48) that follow show how Jesus is indeed the fulfillment of the Old Testament law. The phrase that is repeated constantly in these antitheses, "You have heard that it was said. . . . But I say to you . . . ," establishes Jesus as Lord of the law. In his interpretation, Jesus shows that interior spiritual dispositions have a primary significance over a legalistic interpretation of the law. The examples that Jesus points to (murder, adultery, breaking of oaths, retaliation) all originate from within, from one's heart, from one's intentions. To these interior dispositions one must pay attention. Jesus goes to the very heart of the law and in a way intensifies the demands of the law.

For Jesus, the essence of this law that expresses the fullness of God's will is found in the love commandment (5:43-48). In drawing a contrast with the past, Jesus shows that the new law of love embraces a love for everyone without distinction. This all-embracing love has God, the Father, as its inspiration and example. As children of the heavenly Father, believers imitate God's actions in everything. Just as God, the Father, has expressed an unconditional love for human beings, so human beings are challenged to show the same unconditional love for one another.

In summary, Jesus gives clarity to the spiritual meaning of the law as an expression of God's will for humanity. As Lord of the law, Jesus indicates how the law is to be embraced: not legalistically (as in the case of the scribes and Pharisees), but with an interior disposition. One's heart, one's intentions, are of prime importance. At the center of all law lies the unconditional law of love that reflects God's unconditional love for us human beings.

Spirituality of the Imitation of God:
"Be perfect, just as your heavenly Father is perfect" (5:48)

The call to perfection brings Jesus' teaching on the law to a conclusion. In the Synoptic Gospels the only occurrence of the word "perfect" (*teleios*) is in the Gospel of Matthew (twice here in 5:48 and once at 19:21).[7] While there are many nuances to the concept of "being perfect" (*teleios*) in the Old Testament, the basic meaning conforms to *the idea of completeness or wholeness*. Of all beings, God is without doubt complete and whole. Nothing is lacking in God. When humans are called to be perfect in imitation of God, Jesus is calling them to wholeness and completeness by conforming to God's original will for them. In the antitheses mentioned above, Jesus called his hearers to conform their actions to the original intention that God had for these commands. Jesus' discussion on divorce (5:31-32) illustrates this intention very well. In distinction from Moses, who allowed divorce in certain cases, Jesus calls his hearers to return to God's original intent when he created human beings (Gen 1:27-28 and 2:24).

A further nuance to the concept of "being perfect" appears in the Old Testament and is also obvious here in Matthew. *Perfection entails giving one's heart unconditionally to God.* In the previous passage (5:43-47), the believer was called to love in the same measure that God loves, namely, unconditionally and without distinctions. Later in the sermon (6:25-34), the believer is challenged to total trust in God and to abandon all worries: "Therefore I tell you, do not worry about your life, what you will eat [or drink], or about your body, what you will wear . . ." (6:25). Since God in his providence cares for all creation, how much more will God care for God's children.

The only other place where the word "perfect" (teleios) occurs is in Jesus' discussion with the rich young man (19:16-30) who comes to Jesus and asks, "Teacher, what good must I do to gain eternal life?" (19:16). Jesus responds by stressing the need to keep the commandments, including the command to "love your neighbor as yourself" (19:19). The young man replies that he has led his life in obeying all the commandments. Jesus goes on to show him that there is more to life than a simple legalistic carrying out of the commandments. Jesus says, "If you wish to be perfect . . . ," and challenges him to sell what he has and give the money to the poor, and then come, follow him. Jesus invites the young man to grow spiritually through concern for others, for the poor, for those less privileged than himself. When Jesus challenges him to do something about "this more," he is unable to do so and leaves Jesus' company: "When the young man heard this statement, he went away sad for he had many possessions" (19:22). For this young man, wealth stands in the way of giving himself (his heart) unconditionally to God.

A third nuance to the call "to be perfect" in the Old Testament expresses a wholehearted dedication to God in obedience to God's will. For the people of Israel, obedience was shown through carrying out the stipulations of the law. For the followers of Jesus, obedience to God's will embraces following the way Jesus interpreted the law.[8] For the rich young man, dedication to God and obedience to God required leaving everything and following the Lord. This he could not do.

In Leviticus 19:2, the people of Israel are called to holiness *because* God is holy. In Matthew 5:48, on the other hand, the call to be perfect is *in imitation of* God's actions: "So be perfect, just as your heavenly Father is perfect." Attention is drawn toward the way God treats all humans, even those opposed to him: "For he makes his sun rise on the bad and the good, and causes rain to fall on the just and the unjust" (5:45). Jesus' followers must imitate the same love and compassion God has, especially for their enemies. Believers are called to imitate God's actions, not God's being. *The spirituality of Matthew's gospel is a spirituality of action rather than reflection.* As Jesus states toward the end of the sermon, "Not everyone who says to me, 'Lord, Lord,' will enter the kingdom of heaven, but only the one who does the will of my Father in heaven" (7:21).

Spiritual Ascetical Practices of Almsgiving, Prayer, Fasting (6:1-18)

These three acts of piety (almsgiving, prayer, and fasting) are the foundation for Israel's spiritual life. In the book of Tobit the angel Raphael says, "Prayer and fasting are good, but better than either is almsgiving accompanied by righteousness" (12:8). Righteousness again refers to the human person acting in the way in which God wills. Jesus challenges his disciples: "Unless your righteousness surpasses that of the scribes and Pharisees, you will not enter into the kingdom of heaven" (5:20). A central aspect of Matthew's spirituality emerges here. Human actions are judged by their conformity to God's will as well as by the right intentions of the heart that accompany the actions. When Jesus addresses the pious ascetical practices of almsgiving, prayer, and fasting (6:2-18), his instructions stress that these acts of piety must be performed for the right intentions—one does it because it is God's will.

The traditional Israelite practices of almsgiving, prayer, and fasting were all judged to be of equal value. Jesus, however, places prayer at the center of the Christian spiritual life. By giving an example of prayer, the Lord's Prayer, Jesus shows that prayer enables the believer to embrace the true intentions of doing God's will. The person striving for perfection (5:48) learns that action needs to be inspired by God's grace. Prayer renders action possible. Prayer is not an escape from action or from life. Prayer leads the believer to recognize the demands of the will of the Father as taught by Jesus and to appreciate the grace and strength that comes from this relationship.

Spirituality of Forgiveness

Following the Lord's Prayer, Jesus takes up the saying on forgiveness and illustrates its essential importance. Human forgiveness is a condition for God's forgiveness and expresses the commandment of love. In the Lord's Prayer believers pray, "forgive us our debts, as we forgive our debtors" (6:12). Those who refuse to extend forgiveness to their brothers and sisters cannot expect to receive God's forgiveness.

To illustrate his point about the importance of forgiveness within the community, Jesus teaches a parable on the unforgiving servant in the fourth sermon on the church (18:21-35). Peter asks Jesus, "Lord, if my brother sins against me, how often must I forgive him? As many as seven times?" (18:21). Peter posed this question about forgiveness and then immediately answered it before Jesus could reply! According to the tradition of the rabbis, a person was required to offer forgiveness three times—beyond that no further forgiveness was demanded. No doubt Peter's reference to forgiving "seven times" demonstrates his willingness to go beyond the customary requirement by extending a large measure of forgiveness to those who have caused harm. By referring to "seventy-seven times" (18:22), Jesus stresses that forgiveness should know no limit. The Letter of James also emphasizes the same teaching: "For the judgment is merciless to one who has not shown mercy; mercy triumphs over judgment" (Jas 2:13).

Divine and human forgiveness are interconnected. You cannot have one without the other. In this parable, Jesus illustrates the reason by showing the enormity in the difference between the two debts. The servant owed his master an enormous amount, literally "ten thousand *talents*" (18:24), the equivalent of a laborer's wages for fifteen years! The debt is so vast that the servant has no possibility of ever repaying it. The other servant's debt was minute in comparison, literally "a hundred *denarii*" (18:28), where one *denarius* was the equivalent of a laborer's daily wage. In applying this comparison to the relationship between believers and God, Jesus challenges believers to realize that the enormity of the forgiveness they have received from God is overwhelming. Divine generosity challenges us, believers, to imitate God's forgiving generosity by extending forgiveness to others as God has forgiven us.

Spirituality Rooted in Faith and Expressed in Action (7:24-27)

The Sermon on the Mount concludes with a brief parable whose meaning is articulated at the beginning: those who hear the word must express it in action (7:24, 26). Jesus offers the example of two people who built their houses: one on solid rock, the other on sand. Hearing Jesus' words and acting on them is like the person who built his house on a solid foundation that will endure. On the other hand, the person who refused to act on Jesus' words is like the person who built on shifting sand that would collapse the house.

This conclusion to the sermon connects back to Jesus' teaching on his fulfillment of the law (5:17-20). Jesus had demanded moral action that surpassed that of the scribes and Pharisees. Moral action required one to carry out God's will with the right intentions. The whole Sermon on the Mount breathes a spirituality of faith that must be expressed in action. The spirituality of the Letter of James also embraces at its very heart the importance of faith in action: "So also faith of itself, if it does not have works, is dead" (Jas 2:17).

Our exploration of the Sermon on the Mount has drawn attention to the pulsating heart of the spirituality of the Gospel of Matthew. Most of these spiritual themes recur again in the remaining four sermons. One final parable needs to be considered to bring our exploration of Matthew's spirituality to a conclusion. The last of the parables in the gospel, the parable of the Judgment of the Nations (25:31-46), concludes Jesus' final sermon on the eschatological age (24:1–25:46) and expresses the fundamental spiritual vision all believers should embrace as they strive to put their faith into action. In particular, it clearly illustrates what actions express a believer's faith.

Parable of the Judgment of the Nations (25:31-46)

Spirituality Upholding the Dignity of Every Human Person

This parable brings together much of the essential spiritual vision contained in the Sermon on the Mount and in the gospel as a whole. It provides important insights into Matthew's spirituality.

The parable paints a dramatic picture. At the end of time, "all the nations" are gathered before the judge, the glorious Son of Man (25:31-33), who embraces those whom he calls "blessed" and explains why he invites them to share in his blessedness (25:34-36). Insofar as they performed acts of kindness for "one of these least brothers of mine," they did in fact do them to him (25:34-40). A judgment is also passed on "the accursed," those who refused to perform similar acts of kindness (25:41-45).

The spiritual vision emerges from the two groups mentioned in this parable: "all the nations" (the Gentiles) and "these least brothers of mine" (Jesus' followers). The Gentiles are judged according to the way they treated Jesus' followers who are identified with him. Matthew's gospel had made this identification earlier: "Whoever receives you receives me, and whoever receives me receives the one who sent me" (10:40).

While in the Gospel of Matthew, this parable was meant as a judgment on the nations and how they treated the followers of Jesus, it also applies to the way in which Christians treat others. As Daniel Harrington says:

> If good works to Christians are so important for non-Christians (and non-Jews) to perform, how much more are they to be expected from Christians (and Jews)! If Gentiles are rewarded for good

deeds done to strangers and needy people, so also Christians (and Jews) will be rewarded for such actions.[9]

Reflecting on this parable in this light, a spirituality emerges from this parable that is relevant for all ages: the kindnesses, the help requested, refers to needs everyone can fulfill. What is more ordinary than giving food to the hungry or a drink to the thirsty, making a stranger welcome, visiting the sick and imprisoned? Jesus challenges all people to respond to the immediate needs of those around them. Jesus is not asking people to do dramatic, difficult things. Instead, he challenges his hearers to respond to those in need around them, no matter how small or insignificant the need may be. This spirituality embraces extending kindness into the ordinary situations of daily life.

Further, the help extended to others is spontaneous, not self-seeking. Such responses emerge from a loving, caring heart. Those whom the Son of Man rejects are self-seeking, looking for acknowledgment from others. The same criticism was addressed in the Sermon on the Mount to the scribes and Pharisees who gave alms "to win the praise of others" (6:2). True spirituality is spontaneous, reflecting the essence of one's being, "a generous heart."

Finally, all acts of generosity are ultimately acts that involve Jesus himself. Matthew's gospel had made the identification between Jesus and his followers earlier: "Whoever receives you receives me, and whoever receives me receives the one who sent me" (10:40). Paul's experience of the risen Jesus on the road to Damascus gave him the same realization: "Saul, Saul, why are you persecuting me?" (Acts 9:4). Paul's reflection on the identification between Jesus and those he was persecuting led him to his spiritual vision of the Body of Christ (1 Cor 12:12-31). While the identification here is between Jesus and his followers, identification between God and all human beings is also central to the whole of Scripture. A fundamental insight emerges from the first creation story where human beings are created in God's image and likeness (Gen 1:26-27). All humans bear God's image. All peoples are to be treated with respect because of their identity as being in God's image. This spirituality celebrates the dignity of each individual human person: every Christian as another Christ and every human person as the image of God. A deeper transformation of all human interactions with love as their guide will be the result of such a spirituality.

Matthew's Spirituality Today

Matthew's presentation of Jesus gives us an example of how to make relevant today in the twenty-first century traditions from the past.

Jesus endeavored to appropriate the spirit of the traditions within his Israelite heritage so that they would speak anew to his own people living at another period of time. So it is with the spirituality of Matthew's gospel today. In the same spirit as Jesus we take what Matthew's Jesus has handed onto us. We endeavor to remain faithful to it, while appropriating it for ourselves living in a different world.

Matthew presents a spirituality that centers on *Jesus as "God with us."* God continues to be present with believers of every age through Jesus' spiritual presence: "And behold, I am with you always, until the end of the age" (28:20). As Father, God's spiritual presence is there with believers sustaining and caring for them. God's providential care is there for all creatures, "for he makes his sun rise on the bad and the good, and causes rain to fall on the just and the unjust" (5:45). Believers are in an intimate spiritual relationship with God through Jesus. This relationship is not between equals, but one that acknowledges God's rule over our lives and over our world. This relationship involves a life of service and of humility toward God in which we acknowledge that we are in need of God's guidance and direction—we live our lives dependently upon God knowing that we can only serve one master: "You cannot serve God and mammon" (6:24).

Ours is a world where our common humanity is realized more and more as a result of the technological revolution. What happens in one part of the world is instantly flashed across television screens, the internet, Facebook, Twitter. Instant social networking has brought about a deeper realization today of our common humanity. What affects one part of our global world affects another part. Matthew's spirituality can contribute to this celebration of our common humanity by drawing attention to the responsibilities that emerge from it.

As humans, we are all created in God's image. As Christians, we are united together with Jesus as brothers and sisters in relationship with God as our Father. The implications of this spiritual vision for today's world are significant. Instead of treating those who are different from us as strangers, Matthew's gospel challenges us to see our interconnectedness with all the peoples of the world and to realize the responsibilities that come with this connection.

The parable of the Judgment of the Nations (25:31-46) requires us to respond in the spirit of Jesus to needs in our world wherever they occur. While our first obligation remains to the needs around us, our openness to the wider world enables us to discover needs elsewhere. There are no boundaries where needs are concerned, whether they are famines in

Africa, earthquakes in Haiti and Chile, hurricanes like Katrina, or an oil spill in the Gulf of Mexico. Our common humanity urges us to respond.

Matthew's spirituality embraces *a life led in response to the person of Jesus as "God with us."* This encounter brings with it a transformative experience. We see in the pages of this gospel how the lives of those with Jesus were slowly *transformed.* Their way of life changed whereby they embraced a number of significant and distinctive spiritual aspects. This transformed life is infused by certain characteristic virtues that are motivated by the *imitation of God,* such as love and forgiveness. We imitate God in our actions and dealings with one another: "So, be perfect, just as your heavenly Father is perfect" (5:48). Love and forgiveness are spiritual virtues that our world desperately needs. So many of the problems of our world can only be addressed through attention to these virtues.

In the final analysis, Matthew's spirituality is a *spirituality of faith in action.* The encounter with Jesus transforms our faith to express itself in good deeds. As seen in the final parable of the Judgment of the Nations, the response to the needs and concerns of others occurs spontaneously. In an unconscious way we live out our faith.

Matthew's spirituality witnesses to a *transformed life that embraces an interior spirituality.* Actions are not guided by legalistic interpretations of the law, but by the interior dispositions of the believer. As Jesus indicates in the antitheses (5:21-48), attention must always be given to the interior dispositions of our hearts that give rise to every action. Even in the exercise of the foundational acts of piety and *ascetical practices* such as almsgiving, prayer, and fasting, Jesus stresses that these spiritual practices are to be carried out with the right intentions and interior dispositions. Jesus warns against performing "righteous deeds in order that people may see them" (6:1). Characteristic of young people in today's world is an honesty in acting according to their convictions. *Inwardness* captures the modern person's need to reflect upon his or her own selfhood, a reflection that is distanced from dependence upon others when making decisions. The interior spirituality of Matthew's Jesus provides spiritual material and direction for this interior reflection.

Our exploration of the spirituality of Matthew's gospel shows a spiritual wisdom that transcends the time of the gospel itself. We have much to learn from Matthew's spirituality. Taking Jesus' teaching as a guide for life, we discover a deeper spiritual relationship with God in Jesus. This spiritual relationship transforms our lives and relationships with one another. Our world is in desperate need of such a transformation that can only occur through openness to an encounter with the presence of *God with us.*

CHAPTER THREE

Exploring Mark's Spiritual Vision

While the Gospel of Matthew was the most popular gospel in the early Christian church, interest has shifted to the Gospel of Mark in the modern age. Scholars have identified Mark's gospel as the first gospel to have been written. A careful examination of the relationship between the three gospels Matthew, Mark, and Luke (the Synoptic Gospels) shows that Matthew and Luke used Mark's gospel to construct a gospel for their own communities.

Mark chose the literary genre of a narrative to hand on traditions that he had received about Jesus of Nazareth and his public ministry. A close reading gives the reader the impression that it was written against the backdrop of a period of persecution. Jesus foretells James and John that they will experience suffering in a manner similar to his own. Evidence points to a period when the disciples themselves had been undergoing persecution and suffering: "The cup that I drink, you will drink, and with the baptism with which I am baptized, you will be baptized" (10:39). Further, from the way Mark narrates chapter 13 on the destruction of the temple (13:1-2), the reader gains the impression that this event has recently occurred. As a result of these and other arguments, scholars concluded that Mark's gospel was written shortly after the destruction of Jerusalem and the temple in AD 70 when the sufferings and trauma caused by this event were still vividly in the minds of Jesus' followers and the people of Israel. Many of Jesus' followers had also recently experienced a devastating persecution in Rome imitating Jesus' own sufferings. In Rome, the two most significant leaders, Peter and Paul, had been put to death between AD 64 and 67 during Nero Caesar's persecution of Jesus' followers. Tradition assigns Rome as the place where Mark's gospel was written. All these indications point to Mark's gospel being written from Rome around AD 70.

Matthew's spirituality emerged largely from Jesus' *teaching* and spiritual vision found especially in the five sermons. By contrast, Mark's spirituality is derived from Jesus' *actions*. Mark gives specific attention to the *deeds* of Jesus as a powerful miracle worker. Two characteristics of Mark's gospel are important for understanding his spirituality. The first concerns the *person* of Jesus. In Mark's gospel Jesus is a very enigmatic figure. Mystery surrounds him. Exactly who is Jesus? When concluding some of his miracles, Jesus orders his disciples not to tell anyone about him. For example, when Peter acknowledges, "You are the Messiah," Mark comments, "Then he [Jesus] warned them not to tell anyone about him" (Mark 8:29-30). Scholars have referred to this enigma as the *messianic secret.*

A second characteristic of Mark's gospel that intrigues every reader concerns *discipleship.* Jesus' disciples are presented very differently than they are in Matthew's gospel, where they emerged as good students of Jesus, the Rabbi. In Mark the disciples struggle to understand who Jesus is: "Who then is this whom even wind and sea obey?" (Mark 4:41). An examination of these two intriguing characteristics is key to unlocking Mark's spirituality. We will discover that Mark's gospel is a masterpiece. Mark has deliberately structured his gospel around these two questions in order to capture the interest of his readers and thereby instruct them in the meaning of the person of Jesus and the nature of discipleship. Both aspects are the foundations for Mark's spirituality.

Writing some forty years after Jesus' death and resurrection, Mark tells the account of Jesus' ministry in a way that engages the hearers/readers of his own community and consequently hearers/readers of all time. Mark's gospel presents a spirituality that has enormous importance for hearers/readers of every generation. In examining the spirituality of Mark's gospel, we approach his writing on its own. We intend to remain true to Mark's spiritual vision without making a comparison with the other gospels to avoid being distracted from exploring Mark's spiritual vision faithfully.

Encountering God in the Person of Jesus

God's Action Provides the Framework for Mark's Spirituality

Jesus' ministry is informed by God's action.[1] The gospel opens in the wilderness of Judea with Mark quoting from the prophets Isaiah (40:3) and Malachi (3:1) whom he has linked together in describing John the Baptist. Mark's intention is to show that God's word, spoken through the prophets, now reaches its fulfillment in Jesus' ministry. God's plans, initiated in the Old Testament, are now to be revealed in the person of Jesus. Mark's spirituality is based upon the clear conviction that God's will is sovereign. Since God's plans always come to completion, believers are called to acknowledge God's sovereignty in the world and in their lives. Jesus himself shows his own obedience to God's will in his prayer in the Garden of Gethsemane: "Abba, Father, all things are possible to you. Take this cup away from me, but not what I will but what you will" (Mark 14:36). This prayer illustrates well Jesus' spirituality and it serves as an example for the spirituality of his followers, namely, to place God's will at the forefront of their own lives.

Jesus Speaks and Acts with God's Power as a Further Context for Mark's Spirituality

Jesus' preaching begins with the announcement, "This is the time of fulfillment. The kingdom of God is at hand. Repent, and believe in the gospel" (1:15). From the outset, Jesus' preaching centers on the establishment of God's kingdom. As God's Son (1:1), Jesus' preaching centers on the message of God's kingdom and God's relationship with humanity. Jesus' miracles also center on God's power at work in his actions. Many of Jesus' miracles involving exorcisms of demons reveal an underlying cosmic conflict underway between God's power and that of the devil. When Jesus heals a deaf man, Mark comments that Jesus "looked up to heaven" (7:34), indicating that Jesus' healings derive from God's power. Not only does Jesus preach the message of God's kingdom but he also inaugurates that kingdom through his acts of power. Mark's spirituality challenges his hearers/readers to accept Jesus' invitation to enter God's kingdom by embracing a relationship with the God who rules over their lives.

God speaks on two occasions in the course of this gospel narrative. At Jesus' baptism, God speaks from heaven, acknowledging Jesus as "my beloved Son" (Mark 1:11). This identification of the relationship between God and Jesus at the opening of the gospel authenticates Jesus' ministry. In the middle of the gospel, the voice of God again identifies Jesus as God's Son: "This is my beloved Son. Listen to him" (Mark 9:7). On this occasion, this identification is for the benefit of the disciples. Jesus is about to set off for Jerusalem, where he will be arrested and put to death. God wishes to strengthen the disciples for the time of Jesus' upcoming death. Apart from these two interventions, God is silent. This agrees with the biblical view prominent at this time that God is transcendent and does not intervene directly in human affairs. God acts through intermediaries: in this instance through his Son, Jesus. Mark's spirituality embraces this vision that only through Jesus can one come to know God. Our spirituality today is built upon the same premise: we come to know the divine through the actions and teachings of Jesus.

Spirituality of Encountering the Divine in the Person of Jesus

The opening sentence identifies the gospel's theme: "The beginning of the gospel of Jesus Christ [the Son of God]" (Mark 1:1). Jesus is identified as the Christ (Messiah) and as the Son of God. As Messiah (Christ), Mark presents Jesus as heir to those promises made in the past and recorded in the Old Testament. Jesus is that long-awaited anointed one whom God has sent to establish God's kingdom and bring humanity back into relationship with God. John the Baptist is the fulfillment of Israel's hopes. John is that voice in the wilderness preparing the way for the coming Messiah by "proclaiming a baptism of repentance for the forgiveness of sins" (1:4). As Messiah, Jesus is identified as human. He shares our human nature and understands and appreciates the human context.

In referring to Jesus as "the Son of God"[2] (see also 1:11 and 9:7), Mark identifies Jesus as divine. As human, Mark's spirituality reveals Jesus to be one like us, able to identify with our own situation. As divine, Mark's spirituality reveals Jesus giving us an understanding of God and what God requires of us.

Spiritual Response to Jesus as Messiah, Son of God

Spiritual Values Reflected in Jesus' Journey to Jerusalem (8:22–10:52)

Mark's gospel presents a narrative of Jesus' life and ministry that culminates with his passion and death. The heart of Jesus' spiritual teaching emerges from the central section of the gospel where Jesus is on the way toward Jerusalem to suffering and death (8:22–10:52). During this journey, Jesus instructs his disciples on the spiritual way of life that his followers are to embrace.

A journey was also central to the religious life of the people of Israel. God led them from slavery in Egypt to freedom in the land of Israel. In the course of that journey, God formed them into his own people, giving them his laws (the Ten Commandments) as instructions on how to lead their lives in relationship to their God. The same thought operates here in Jesus' journey with his followers. On this journey, Jesus also instructs his followers on their relationship with God and with himself. He prepares them for his death on behalf of humanity (10:45) and challenges them to accept suffering and death in their own lives.

Mark has structured this narrative of Jesus' journey toward Jerusalem (8:22–10:52) in a most revealing way[3] that enables us to explore his spirituality. Mark's spiritual teaching is framed within two episodes where Jesus heals two physically blind people (8:22-26; 10:46-52). In the opening episode, the *blind beggar at Bethsaida* has his sight restored by Jesus in two stages. At first the beggar sees vaguely: "I see people looking like trees and walking" (8:24). A second time Jesus touched his eyes and "his sight was restored and he could see everything distinctly" (8:25). This physical healing of the beggar's sight is contrasted with the spiritual blindness of the disciples. In this section, Jesus struggles to bring them to spiritual insight and faith in him. Their fixation with their own understanding of who Jesus is lies at the center of the disciples' spiritual blindness. On three occasions, Jesus explains directly to them that he is going to Jerusalem, where he will suffer and be put to death. But, their spiritual blindness prevents them from grasping what Jesus is telling them.

Following the first healing of a blind person, Mark narrates Peter's confession at Caesarea-Philippi (8:27–9:1) that marks a turning point in the gospel. In this northernmost part of the country, Jesus asks his followers, "Who do people say that I am?" (8:27). Peter replies first and acknowledges, "You are the Messiah" (8:29). At issue here are different understandings of the Messiah. Peter, as all his contemporaries did, was hoping for the coming of a Messiah who would be like another King David and establish God's kingly rule over the people of Israel. In doing so, this Messiah would overthrow Roman rule and establish God's kingdom.

This was certainly not Jesus' vision. While his preaching and ministry did aim at the establishment of God's kingdom, the nature of God's rule was in the spiritual realm, not the political. This episode explains why Jesus told his disciples here and elsewhere to keep quiet about him (8:30). He distanced himself from the political hopes associated with the concept of Messiah. In challenging Peter's idea of Messiah, Jesus gave his ministry a clearer understanding. His was a spiritual ministry focused on bringing true salvation to humanity through his suffering, death, and resurrection (8:31-33).

Jesus does more than reveal his own identity and mission. He instructs the disciples on the spiritual values that should guide their lives (8:34–9:1). In this first announcement of his death and resurrection, Jesus challenges his followers to abandon all desire for power. Their discipleship would entail accepting the cross, as Jesus did. Their willingness to lose their lives for Jesus' sake would ultimately bring them salvation. Jesus envisages martyrdom for himself and for those who follow him.

In the following episode of the *transfiguration (9:2-8), the spiritual blindness of the disciples continues.* The transfiguration gave Jesus' disciples a glimpse into his true identity. Jesus appeared together with Moses and Elijah, representing the Law and the Prophets respectively. In a symbolic way, their presence showed that the whole Old Testament was leading to Jesus. As happened at the baptism, a voice from heaven proclaimed Jesus to be the Son of God: "This is my beloved Son. Listen to him" (9:7). We, the readers, understand Jesus' identity clearly. But, the disciples still fail to understand. As they descend the mountain, they continue to show their spiritual blindness as they discuss among themselves what Jesus' speech about this rising from the dead could mean (9:10).

When Jesus speaks about his impending death a second time (9:30-32), Mark comments, "But they did not understand the saying, and they were afraid to question him" (9:32). As the disciples journeyed along the road (9:33-37), they argued among themselves "who was the greatest" (9:34)! Rather than focusing on the cost to Jesus and the spiritual significance of his death, the disciples were concerned about their own status and ambitions. Jesus' response draws attention to his spiritual values that are in sharp contrast to those of his disciples. To be a follower of Jesus means emulating Jesus' own spiritual values. For society of that time, the most important values were status, wealth, power. In contrast, Jesus teaches the countercultural spiritual value of service: "If anyone wishes to be first, he shall be the last of all and the servant of all" (9:35). To reinforce this spiritual vision, Jesus holds up a child for imitation. In the context of their society, children were considered to be among the lowest members. Jesus uses a child to symbolize his total concern for the lowest: "Whoever receives one child such as this in my name, receives me; and whoever receives me, receives not me but the One who sent me" (9:37). Again Jesus proposes a spiritual value that is countercultural: concern for those whom society regards as insignificant.

On a third occasion, Jesus speaks about his death (10:32-34). Attention is given again to the disciples' response (10:35-45). James and John request Jesus to let them sit on his right and left hand when he comes into his kingdom. Seats on the right and left of a king were privileged places occupied by those who shared the king's power. James and John again show their spiritual blindness. They are unable to let go of their preconceived notions that rested on power and prestige.

Jesus takes this opportunity to focus on his spiritual values. Using the metaphor of a cup to refer to his suffering, and baptism to refer to his death and resurrection, Jesus tells James and John that they will indeed share his suffering and death. For Jesus, the most important values in his kingdom are service and the willingness to follow him into suffering and death and not, as society celebrates, the desire for positions of power and prestige. Presenting himself as an example, Jesus speaks of his mission in this way: "For the Son of Man did not come to be served but to serve and to give his life as a ransom for many" (10:45).

The narrative of the journey to Jerusalem culminates in a second *healing of a blind person, Bartimaeus (10:46-52)*. Together with the previous miracle of the healing of the blind man at Bethsaida (8:22-26), this passage frames the journey to Jerusalem and invites us, the readers, to reflect on the previous material that had focused on the three predictions of Jesus' suffering, death, and resurrection. Whereas we, the readers, have understood that Jesus' mission would be carried out through suffering and death, the disciples still continue to remain spiritually blind to the true meaning of Jesus as Messiah. Jesus' conflict with his disciples serves as a mirror for us readers to see reflected those true spiritual values that we, as Jesus' followers, should embrace. Jesus calls his disciples both then and now to embrace a spirituality stamped by a willingness to embrace the cross of sacrifice, suffering, and death (8:34; 10:38-39); an openness to embrace those whom society ignores (9:36-37); and a life characterized by service (9:35; 10:43-45).

Spirituality of Prayer Expressed as Trust in God

Mark's gospel offers Jesus' followers further spiritual values. Throughout his life Jesus demonstrates total trust in his Father. Such trust serves as an example for his disciples in their own lives. Jesus' faith and trust in the Father is expressed above all in prayer. As Mark's Jesus says, "Have faith in God. Amen, I say to you, whoever says to this mountain, 'Be lifted up and thrown into the sea,' and does not doubt in his heart but believes that what he says will happen, it shall be done for him. Therefore I tell you, all that you ask for in prayer, believe that you will receive it and it shall be yours" (11:22-24).

In the *Garden of Gethsemane*, Jesus spends his last hours in prayer to his Father. This prayer offers a wonderful paradigm for his followers to imitate: "Abba, Father, all things are possible to you. Take this cup away from me, but not what I will but what you will" (14:36). Jesus' prayer shows a fundamental element of all true prayer: an openness that accepts God's will. As a paradigm for prayer, Jesus illustrates the spiritual attitude all believers should adopt in their own prayer life. While it is important to make known our needs and desires to God, we must also recognize that God has a plan. Our requests to God must always be tempered, as Jesus shows, by an openness to God's will. Jesus' prayer in the Garden of Gethsemane shows he did not want to die. Nevertheless, Jesus accepts God's will: "not what I will but what you will" (14:36). The above two passages on prayer need to be harmonized if we are to appropriate in our lives Jesus' insight into prayer. Jesus encourages us to make known to his Father our concerns. By prayer, we show our trust and dependence on God (see above, 11:22-24). At the same time, we acknowledge that all prayer needs to be expressed "according to God's will."

Spirituality of Following Jesus in Service

For Mark's Jesus, the two essential spiritual characteristics of a disciple are those of *following* and *service.* Jesus calls the first disciples, Peter, Andrew, James, and John, in these simple words: "'Come after me, and I will make you fishers of men.' Then they left their nets and *followed* him" (1:17). By following Jesus, they are in a privileged position. They learn from him directly and absorb his way of life. At the end of the gospel narrative, when the disciples have all abandoned Jesus, the only people remaining are a group of women. Mark comments, "There were also women looking on from a distance. Among them were Mary Magdalene, Mary the mother of the younger James and of Joses, and Salome. These women had *followed* him when he was in Galilee and ministered to him" (15:40-41). Mark shows the essence of a true disciple is to have been with Jesus, to have "followed" him. Mark's gospel opens and closes on this need to be with Jesus and to learn from him. The same is true for every believer. While Jesus is no longer physically on earth, he is still spiritually present with his disciples. We are called to remain spiritually connected to the Lord Jesus and to learn from him. That spiritual connection enables the believer to continue to follow Jesus and receive the spiritual guidance and support necessary to lead life as a true disciple.

Mark's focus at the end of the narrative on this spiritual response of this group of women who continue to faithfully "follow" Jesus is a way of highlighting that *the call to follow Jesus is embraced by all people, especially those whom the society of the day tended to ignore.* The gospel gives attention to the following of Jesus by fishermen, tax collectors, sinners (2:13-17). As Mark's Jesus explains when criticized for associating with certain groups of people, "Those who are well do not need a physician, but the sick do. I did not come to call the righteous but sinners" (2:17). At the end of the narrative as well, a Roman centurion confesses, "Truly this man was the Son of God!" (15:39). At the opening of his narrative, Mark had announced his intention of demonstrating that Jesus was the Son of God (1:1). The only person to acknowledge Jesus as Son of God is unexpectedly a Roman centurion. Once again Mark illustrates that the spiritual response to Jesus' message moves in unexpected ways. All people are called to become believers and to respond in faith and love to God's action working in their lives. The mention of the Roman soldier here has universal significance. This message of Mark's gospel is as relevant today as it was then. People of all walks of life, especially the poor and marginalized among society, respond spiritually to Jesus' message.

Service is without doubt the most important spiritual virtue that Jesus requires of a disciple. We have already seen the importance Jesus gave to service in his three discussions with his disciples concerning his approaching death. He challenged them to abandon their earthly hopes of attaining power by stressing the need to be at the service of others. Jesus gives himself as the example of one who serves others to the point of death: "For the Son of Man did not come to be served but to serve and to give his life as a ransom for many" (10:45). Although the disciples had been with Jesus for a lengthy period, they still struggled to grasp that service was the hallmark of a true follower.

In contrast, Mark illustrates how women did grasp that service was the foundation for a disciple's life. At the beginning of the gospel, Mark draws attention to the importance of service as a response to Jesus' compassion. When Jesus heals Peter's mother-in-law, Mark comments that Jesus "approached, grasped her hand, and helped her up. Then the fever left her and *she waited on them*" (1:31). This translation in the New American Bible, "she waited on," is unfortunate because it loses the full sense of what Jesus' message requires. The Greek verb for "she waited on" is *diakonein*, which means "to serve." Mark shows at the outset of his narrative that the true response to Jesus' actions in the lives of his followers is *service*. Peter's mother-in-law understood this by responding to Jesus' compassionate healing through an act of service. While her response of "waiting on them" may have involved cooking a meal for Jesus, Mark draws attention to much more than this. He shows that her action is essentially an action of service—the response called forth from every follower.

At the end of the narrative, Mark shows a group of women whose lives again embody the true response to Jesus. In the scene where three women are watching the crucifixion from afar (15:40-41), Mark commented that when they used to follow Jesus in Galilee, "they *ministered* to him" (15:41). Once again, the New American Bible fails to capture the spiritual message that Mark intends. The word translated as "ministered" is again the verb *diakonein*. By beginning and ending his gospel (1:31 and 15:41) with the same spiritual idea of service, Mark highlights the key response required to Jesus' actions in a disciple's life. Mark also notes that women disciples were the ones to grasp this, while the male disciples failed to do so. These women disciples become for us today true examples of what it means to be a disciple: to dedicate our lives in service as a response to God working in our lives. Just as Jesus' whole life was one of service, so our lives, led in imitation of him (and of the first women disciples), must also be lives of service of Jesus and of one another.

Countercultural Spirituality

From the outset of the gospel, Jesus' spiritual message is set against the values and spirit of the society in which he and his followers lived. The picture of John the Baptist portrays a person at home in the wilderness—he had left behind the usual customary world of villages and the city: "John was clothed in camel's hair, with a leather belt around his waist. He fed on locusts and wild honey" (1:6). God had chosen John to prepare the way for the coming of his Anointed One. John falls victim to the establishment because he had criticized the ruler, Herod Antipas: "It is not lawful for you to have your brother's wife" (6:18). John's criticisms challenged the political establishment and as a consequence he was executed. John's death foreshadows Jesus' death. Jesus too was embroiled in controversies with the religious establishment. He saw that the religious establishment operated with a strict legalistic mindset that regulated all people's actions. Jesus was constantly criticized, especially by the Pharisees, for breaking the Sabbath day. He showed a depth of spiritual insight into the way in which laws should be obeyed. Commenting on the Sabbath observance, Jesus says, "The sabbath was made for man, not man for the sabbath. That is why the Son of Man is lord even of the sabbath" (2:27-28). Jesus points to the purpose of law: it is there for the good of mankind, not vice versa. Jesus invokes a spiritual attitude for the fulfillment of law that is relevant for all generations and for all times. Laws are made for the spiritual welfare of humanity. Like Jesus, one is not to embrace a legalistic attitude to the fulfillment of laws. Instead, Jesus promotes a spirituality that gives attention first and foremost to the needs of others over the legalistic fulfillment of laws.

The countercultural nature of Mark's spirituality centers on Jesus' acceptance of his imminent death and his stress that his own disciples must take up their own cross and follow him (8:34-38). The spirituality of a disciple is characterized by the imitation of Christ (*imitatio Christi*). While the world's values embrace the need for power, wealth, and status, Jesus' spiritual values are exactly the opposite (8:35-36). Jesus challenges believers of all times to embrace a spiritual way of life that seeks to place Jesus and the imitation of his life at the very center of their lives in contrast to an earthly way of life that sets out to find happiness and meaning in temporal things that soon disappear. This imitation of the way of Jesus demands a commitment to renounce one's own self and to embrace the cross that may even lead to death. For all believers, their spirituality of commitment to the person of Christ contrasts with that selfish life that strives to satisfy every earthly need. A life set on fulfilling material needs will end ultimately in destruction, while a life centered on the imitation of Jesus will bring the fullness of life.

Spirituality Formed by the Cross

The shadow of the cross hangs over the entire gospel. Mark's gospel comprises some sixteen chapters. More than one-third of the gospel is devoted to the last week in Jesus' life. In chapter 11:1 Jesus enters Jerusalem and begins a final week that culminates in death the following Friday (15:22-41) and resurrection three days later on early Sunday morning (16:1-8). But, the focus on the cross begins earlier with Jesus' long journey to Jerusalem (8:22–10:52), a journey to suffering and death. During this journey, as we have seen, Jesus foretold his suffering and death on three occasions (8:31; 9:31; 10:33-34). This means that one-half of Mark's gospel is focused on Jesus' suffering and death. Added to these observations, we note that early in his gospel Mark describes John the Baptist's death (6:17-29) as a foreshadowing of Jesus' death. The one who prepared the way for Jesus (1:2-11) also prepared the way for Jesus' death. John was beheaded because of his moral criticism of the authority of the day; Jesus was condemned to death because he had aroused opposition from religious and political authorities.

Without doubt *the spirituality of Mark's gospel is shaped totally by the cross of Jesus.* It is a spirituality that proclaims a Christian way of life for all believers. Mark's gospel is more than a simple narrative about Jesus' death. Mark narrates the passion and death of Jesus for *the purpose of invoking a spiritual response to Jesus' suffering from his readers.*

Not only did Mark's Jesus foretell the suffering and death of James and John (10:38-40) but he also challenged every disciple to realize that following him meant the willingness to embrace the cross in their own lives: "He summoned the crowd with his disciples and said to them, 'Whoever wishes to come after me must deny himself, take up his cross, and follow me'" (8:34-35). Discipleship involves identifying with Jesus, an identification that embraces an openness to follow him along the same path to suffering and death. Jesus' suffering and death led to the glory of the resurrection. The same path is assured his followers. Mark's spirituality is indeed shaped by the cross and speaks especially to believers who are experiencing rejection and persecution in their adherence to Jesus, to their faith in him and his message. This spirituality, shaped by the cross, speaks to every Christian in every age. Fidelity to Jesus and to the message of the gospel always brings with it sacrifices and hardships. By embracing these in Jesus' name, believers identify with the mystery of his suffering, death, and resurrection. Suffering is not the end, but the prelude to resurrection. As Jesus' death was transformed through the glory of the resurrection, so everyone who follows him in suffering and death is promised a similar transformation into resurrected life.

Mark's Spirituality Today

Throughout this chapter attention has been drawn to aspects of Mark's gospel that are undoubtedly significant for today's spiritual life. Significant spiritual values emerge from Mark's narrative. Essentially, these values are as countercultural today as they were in Jesus' day: placing trust in God rather than in one's own efforts, establishing a relationship with God through prayer, following Jesus in service rather than in establishing one's own importance.

However, the central aspect of the spirituality of Mark's gospel lies in *the centrality of the cross.* Why does Mark's narrative focus so dominantly on the suffering and death of Jesus? The answer lies in the context and background to Mark's narrative. A critical analysis of Mark's gospel supports the view of tradition that Mark was written in Rome shortly after the deaths of Paul and Peter and the persecution that broke out under Emperor Nero (54–68) in Rome against Christians.[4] Mark is writing to strengthen his own readers in this time of persecution. In doing so, he provides a narrative that gives strength and support to all Christians who are experiencing suffering and persecution. It is indeed a *spirituality for martyrs*. Mark's Jesus points to the disciples James and John, and says that their following will result in embracing the suffering of the cup and the baptism of death and resurrection. What Jesus says to them he intends for all his followers (10:38-40). Those early followers of Jesus struggled to make sense of the suffering of their master. Mark points to a later period when they came to face persecution in their own lives. Their spirituality had been strengthened through Jesus' resurrection and they in turn were able to remain faithful while facing their own struggles and suffering. For Christians at every age, the Gospel of Mark provides strength and encouragement on their spiritual journey as they strive to imitate Christ when they also experience suffering.

As readers and modern-day disciples of Jesus, we are invited to accept the cross on the path of discipleship. Christians in North America and Europe tend to forget that martyrdom for one's faith continues today in our world. In preparation for the jubilee year 2000, Pope John Paul II drew attention to this fact when he wrote in his apostolic letter *Tertio Millennio Adveniente*:

> *In our own century the martyrs have returned*, many of them nameless, *"unknown soldiers"* as it were *of God's great cause*. As far as possible, their witness should not be lost to the Church.[5]

For these martyrs, the spirituality of Mark's gospel was as relevant as it was for Christians of the first century.

For Christians living in the twenty-first century and not faced with physical persecution and death, the spirituality of Mark's gospel still remains relevant. Christians face the daily ridicule that the modern world often heaps upon them either individually or as a group in the media or in the workplace. We are also challenged by Mark's spirituality to embrace our own individual sufferings and daily hardships. We are asked to accept whatever form the cross may take in our daily lives. More important, we are called to identify with all those who are suffering in our world and in society around us. We identify with the lowly and the suffering of our world; we distance ourselves from anything that might lead to supremacy over others. We strive as well to live out Jesus' countercultural values. In imitation of Jesus, in service of one another, in the trust we place in Jesus and God, Mark's gospel proposes a spirituality that enters into the mystery of the cross and provides confidence in the firm belief that it is only through the cross that we come to experience the resurrection.

CHAPTER FOUR

Exploring Luke's Spiritual Vision

The Gospel of Luke and the Acts of the Apostles form two parts of one major work (Luke-Acts). In the ancient world, manuscripts were produced in the form of scrolls made from the papyrus plant. The standard Greek scroll was about thirty-five feet in length. Consequently, long writings would of necessity be divided into two parts. Originally the writer, Luke, produced a unified work that he broke into two parts for the sake of convenience.[1]

The opening verses of the Gospel of Luke (1:1-4) and the Acts of the Apostles (1:1-3) demonstrate the original unity of Luke-Acts. Both writings begin in the first person ("I") and they are addressed to the same important person ("most excellent Theophilus"). Acts deliberately refers back to the gospel as, "In the first book." Furthermore, Acts summarizes briefly the contents of the gospel. Placed together, the two volumes make up about one-quarter of the whole New Testament. In his prologue (1:3-4), Luke acknowledges that he was not one of Jesus' original disciples. He assures his hearers/readers, however, that his knowledge of Jesus and of his message is trustworthy since it is based on authentic traditions he had received from "eyewitnesses from the beginning and ministers of the word" (1:2). All this points to a gospel that was written for third-generation believers living toward the end of the first Christian century."

While the Gospel of Matthew was certainly the most popular gospel in early Christianity, the Gospel of Luke captures the popular imagination of present-day Christians. Our vision of the Christmas scene is largely imprinted with stories and pictures emanating from the infancy account in Luke's gospel. Scenes on Christmas cards, portraying the birth of the child Jesus lying in a manger with animals surrounding him, owe their inspiration to Luke's narrative. Some of the most well-known parables come from the Gospel of Luke (the Good Samaritan [10:29-37] and the Prodigal Son [15:11-32]).

Like Matthew, Luke based himself on the Gospel of Mark and the Sayings Source Q. He also had access to a source specific to himself. While Matthew placed the Q Sayings within the context of five sermons to illustrate Jesus as Teacher, Luke placed them in the context of Jesus' journey toward Jerusalem. Mark had narrated the account of Jesus' journey to Jerusalem in two and a half chapters (8:22–10:52). Luke expanded Mark's original journey to a full ten chapters (9:51–19:27) to illustrate his theological understanding of Jesus' teaching and ministry for the wider Greco-Roman world.

Luke's gospel embraces a clear theological-historical vision. Luke situates Jesus within a specific historical framework. Jesus' birth occurred during the rule of Augustus Caesar (2:1-2). The preaching activity of John the Baptist took place "in the fifteenth year of the reign of Tiberius Caesar" (3:1-2). Besides locating Jesus' birth and ministry within the historical world of the Roman Empire, Luke also situates Jesus' ministry within the vast plan of God's salvation for the human race. Luke's vision of God's dealings with humanity is of epic proportions. His outlook embraces three time periods: the *period of Israel* when God chose that nation as God's own and made known to them God's plan for the salvation of humanity, the *period of Jesus* that brings this plan of salvation to fulfillment, and the *period of the church* when the apostles extended this salvation beyond Israel to the peoples of the world.

Luke-Acts embraces these three time periods. The gospel opens with John the Baptist, who belongs to the period of Israel. *Jesus' ministry* lies at the center of this plan to bring salvation to the world. The Acts begins the period of the church with the account of Jesus' ascension and traces how this salvation that Jesus won for humanity was extended through the teaching of his followers to the "ends of the earth" (Acts 1:8). While most of the spiritual themes within the Gospel of Luke are carried forward into the Acts of the Apostles, this chapter will limit its reflections to the gospel for the sake of brevity.

Encountering the God of Salvation in the Person of Jesus

As has been stressed, spirituality embraces an understanding and experience of God that requires a response. The heart of Luke's spirituality embraces the vision that God is a God of salvation. God expressed that salvation in the past through Israel and now God communicates this salvation to humanity in a unique way through his Son, Jesus. His followers continue Jesus' work by extending his salvation to all humanity.

The Time of Fulfillment

According to Luke, the time of Jesus fulfills the time of Israel ("the events that have been fulfilled among us . . ." [1:1]). The birth, life, and ministry of Jesus are a fulfillment of what God had done and said in the past. In his inaugural sermon at his home town of Nazareth (4:16-30), Jesus read from the prophet Isaiah. In concluding the reading, he acknowledged that "today this scripture passage is fulfilled in your hearing" (4:21). Jesus identified this passage from Isaiah as referring to his ministry: what God had promised in the past to Israel is now being realized. For Jesus, the outreach to the poor and marginalized of society captured the essence of God's prior message to Israel. Now Jesus continues to share God's concern and empathy for the marginalized.

John the Baptist Heralds This Time of Fulfillment

In chapters 1 and 2 Luke narrates the account of the births of John and Jesus in a parallel way. By making this visual comparison, Luke shows that John's birth prepares the way for Jesus' birth. At the same time, Jesus' birth overshadowed that of John. John represents the past—Jesus fulfills that past. This same image of John and his relationship with Jesus runs throughout this gospel narrative. After this infancy narrative, the gospel follows Mark but introduces John in a much fuller way. John's role remains the same: as a representative of the past, he prepares the way for Jesus. Quoting the prophet Isaiah (40:3-5), John calls out:

> "A voice of one crying out in the desert:
> 'Prepare the way of the Lord,
>   make straight his paths.
> Every valley shall be filled
>   and every mountain and hill shall be made low.
> The winding roads shall be made straight,
>   and the rough ways made smooth,
> and all flesh shall see the salvation of God.'" (3:4-6)

Luke's John uses this prophecy to show John's role in preparing the way for Jesus, whose coming will be the fulfillment of the great hopes of Israel's past. However, he tweaks the words of the prophecy to conclude that in the person of Jesus "all flesh shall see the salvation of God" (3:6). Luke uses the quotation of Isaiah to stress Jesus' mission of bringing salvation to all peoples.

Within the world of Israel, John points to the new age about to burst forth with Jesus' coming. Yet, John belongs to the past. Jesus emphasizes this point later in the gospel when he says of John, "The law and the prophets lasted until John . . ." (16:16). While John may be the greatest person to have lived in the time of Israel (7:28), he marks a transition to a new time period. Those who belong to Jesus' kingdom are greater than John because Jesus inaugurates a new relationship with God through the gift of salvation attained through his death and resurrection.

The Time of Jesus Is the Fulfillment of God's Gift of Salvation

In the infancy narrative (chaps. 1–2), the significance of Jesus' birth centers around God's promises of salvation. A cursory glance at these two chapters shows almost every event celebrating God's salvation. Mary's song (the *Magnificat* [1:46-55]) reflects her spirit of joy and humility at God's choice of her to be the mother of the Savior. She opens by saying, "My soul proclaims the greatness of the Lord; my spirit rejoices in God my *savior*" (1:46-47). After the birth of John the Baptist, Zechariah also bursts out in a song of praise (the *Benedictus* [1:68-79]): "Blessed be the Lord, the God of Israel, for he has visited and brought *redemption* to his people. He has raised up a horn for our *salvation* within the house of David his servant" (1:68-69). The announcement of Jesus' birth to the shepherds in the fields continues this celebration of God's salvation: "Do not be afraid; for behold, I proclaim to you good news of great joy that will be for all the people. For today in the city of David a *savior* has been born for you who is Messiah and Lord" (2:10-11).

While the songs of Mary and Zechariah celebrate God's salvation for the people of Israel, the "righteous and devout" Simeon proclaims another song (the *Nunc Dimittis*) in the temple. Simeon prophesies that God's salvation is intended for all people, not just the people of Israel, "a light for revelation to the Gentiles, and glory for your people Israel" (2:29-32). Simeon celebrates the centrality of this new time of Jesus where God's salvation is destined for the whole human race. Another person, Anna, a prophetess, is also in the temple precincts and she too reinforces this gift of God's salvation in the person of the child Jesus: "And coming forward at that very time, she gave thanks to God and spoke about the child to all who were awaiting the *redemption* of Jerusalem" (2:38).

The spirituality of Luke's gospel centers upon this understanding of God as the God of salvation for Israel and for the entire world. According to Luke, this salvation that Jesus brings touches every aspect of life for every human person. Salvation intends not simply a deliverance from sin, but a gift from God that overcomes every form of evil in the lives of people.

In his ministry, Jesus encounters people in their daily struggles: the poor, the outcasts of society, those suffering both physically and mentally. In every dimension of the human condition, Jesus reaches out with compassion to touch people where they are struggling the most. In every instance, they encounter God's grace of salvation in his person. In the course of his ministry, Jesus struggles with the devil, who attempts to withstand God's gift of salvation. With Jesus' death on the cross, it appears at first that the devil has won. But, with God raising Jesus from the dead, God's salvation triumphs.

God's salvation, encountered in the person of Jesus, is not limited to the period of the gospel narrative. God's salvation is intended to touch every dimension of people's lives at all times, in all places. The gospel provides a paradigm that shows people encountering God's salvation in Jesus, especially in those moments of life where they experience and struggle with every aspect of evil. The paradigm speaks to every believer of every age. Luke's spirituality shows that every believer, in their darkest struggles, can encounter God's salvation in the person of Jesus. God continues to offer salvation. God continues to touch our lives through the grace he showers upon us through the death and resurrection of Jesus that is extended to us through his church as the Acts will show. God's salvation, God's grace, is to be experienced not just in the future life of heaven, but more especially at every moment of each person's existence as a member of God's kingdom in a special relationship with "God my Savior" (1:47), as Mary proclaims.

Spiritual Response to Jesus as Universal Savior

A Journey Spirituality

The spiritual implications of God's salvation offered us in the person of Jesus are illustrated more fully in the course of Jesus' journey to Jerusalem. Luke found in the Gospel of Mark an account of Jesus' journey to Jerusalem (8:22–10:52) that marked the turning point in the ministry of the suffering Messiah. Taking material from the Q Sayings Source, Luke expanded that original narrative in Mark to a full ten chapters (9:51–19:27). He used this long journey to Jerusalem to communicate the essence and importance of Jesus' spiritual teaching for his disciples. The *journey* is a well-known literary device found within the world of the Israelites and the peoples of Greece and Rome. During the forty-year journey from slavery in Egypt to liberation in Canaan (the exodus), God formed the people of Israel into God's own nation through the gift of the covenant. The stipulations of the covenant (chief among them were the Ten Commandments) expressed the essence of God's will and how they were to respond to God in their daily actions. God also journeyed with them to protect and guide them along the way.

For the peoples of Greece and Rome, journeys also lay at the foundation of their consciousness. Homer's *Odyssey* describes Odysseus's ten-year journey from the destruction of Troy to his eventual return home on the island of Ithaca. Some of the gods journey with Odysseus and he discovers throughout his journey their will for him and their continued protection, assistance, and guidance. In a similar vein, the *Aeneid* uses the motif of a journey to show Aeneas, prince of Troy, journeying from the ashes of Troy to the Italian peninsula where he and his men established their settlements that were to become the ancestors of the glorious race of Romans. They were aided, protected, and guided by their own Trojan gods.

The readers and hearers of Luke's gospel would have been very familiar with all these journey narratives. Luke deliberately embraces this motif. During the journey with his disciples to Jerusalem, Jesus instructs them in his spiritual teachings. An examination of these ten chapters illustrates well the responses that Jesus' spiritual teachings on God's salvation require of believers. For every reader of the Gospel of Luke, a journey spirituality would immediately speak to their own life's journey. The spirituality that emerges from this journey shows that God journeys with every believer and how they are called to respond.

Spirituality of Unconditional Response

At the outset of the journey, three people approach Jesus and ask to follow him (9:57-62). When Jesus demanded an unqualified response, each raised some obstacle to their following. Jesus replied that nothing must distract from an immediate response, not even obligations such as the burial of a parent. From such graphic illustrations, Jesus showed that the response must be immediate and total. This sets out the radical nature of Jesus' spirituality for every age of the Christian church. The following of Jesus is never meant to be half-hearted, or conditional. It is always a full life-giving response.

Spirituality Founded upon Love

As Matthew and Mark do, Luke records Jesus' teaching on the love commandment (10:25-28). A scholar of the law asks Jesus, "Teacher, what must I do to inherit eternal life?" (10:25). Jesus turns the question back on the scholar who answers by quoting the love of God and love of neighbor (10:27). To illustrate what real love is, Jesus offers two illustrations.

In the parable of the Good Samaritan (10:29-37), Jesus addresses the second dimension of the love command: love of neighbor. Jesus tells the story of a man attacked by robbers in the course of a journey. Those one would expect to aid this victim (the priest and the Levite) ignore him. Only the Samaritan (whom the people of Israel despised) responded and offered the injured man whatever assistance he could give. Here is a remarkable story of love for a neighbor. The Samaritan demonstrates the true qualities of love. Love knows *no boundaries*: the Samaritan (whom society regarded as an enemy) offers assistance to a person from Israel. Love also demands *sacrifice*: the Samaritan pays for the traveler's recuperation. Love expects *nothing in return*: the Samaritan pays without asking for anything in return. Jesus' command to the scholar of the law is applicable to the spiritual journey of every person of faith: "Go and do likewise" (10:37). Do likewise in demonstrating love for God and love for one's neighbor. As Fulton Sheen wrote:

> Our Lord made neighborhood coextensive with humanity. Any human being is a neighbor who needs aid or to whom one can render aid. A neighbor is not one bound by the same race, nor is he the one close to us. He may be the one farthest away: he could even be an enemy.[2]

In the next episode (10:38-42), Luke describes Jesus' encounter with his friends Martha and Mary to show the other dimension of the love command: love of God. Martha spends her time away from Jesus, preparing the meal. Mary ignores her sister's hard work. She is captivated with being in Jesus' presence. A spirituality defined by love of God demands being in God's presence. Love of God embraces one's whole being. One is enraptured and absorbed in God's presence where all distractions end. Confronting a choice between service of others and love of God, the follower of Jesus will always choose the place at the feet of Jesus, as Mary did.

Spirituality Directed by Prayer

In Luke's gospel, Jesus is defined as a man of prayer. Before all the important moments in his life, the reader sees Jesus at prayer: after his baptism (3:21); before he chooses the Twelve, he spends the night in prayer (6:12). In the course of the journey to Jerusalem, Luke notes how Jesus "was praying in a certain place" (11:1). When the disciples see Jesus at prayer, they ask him to teach them how to pray. Just as Jesus demonstrated the need to be in spiritual union with his Father, especially in the decisive moments of life, so the disciples seek to discover their own path to spiritual union with the Father. Jesus' example is important for the spirituality of every follower at every age.

In response to his disciples' request, Jesus teaches his followers the Lord's Prayer (11:2-4). In the Gospel of Matthew, Jesus gave this prayer in the context of the Sermon on the Mount. Luke, on the other hand, has incorporated it within the journey to stress the importance of prayer in the everyday lives of his followers. This prayer should be viewed as a "communal prayer," not an individual prayer. The disciples as a group had asked Jesus to teach them to pray. In the prayer, Jesus directs the petitions toward a union with all the members of the community: "Give *us* each day . . ." (11:3). In teaching his disciples this prayer, Jesus presents them with an example containing the essential elements: the concept of God as Father, who sustains believers along their spiritual journey (11:3); the prayer for God's forgiveness that in turn demands the willingness to extend that same forgiveness to all who cause one harm (11:4); and the prayer for God's protection in the time of the final test (11:4).

Not only does Luke's Jesus give his disciples an example of prayer but he also stresses certain qualities that should define a believer's prayer life. To illustrate the importance of *persistence* in prayer Jesus offers the parable of the friend who comes at midnight (11:5-8): "I tell you, if he does not get up to give him the loaves because of their friendship, he will get up to give him whatever he needs because of his persistence" (11:8). Likewise, Jesus' followers must not become easily discouraged. Their spirituality must embrace persistence in making their prayers known to God. A further parable on the persistence of prayer occurs later in the journey: the persistence of a widow in petitioning an unjust judge (18:1-8).

Confidence in being heard by the Father is a further quality marking a disciple's prayer (11:9-13). Just as a human father knows what is good for his child, so the heavenly Father responds by offering the disciple what is needed most, the gift of the Holy Spirit (11:13). God's Spirit enlivens Christian believers in their relationship with God as Father and strengthens them on their spiritual journey.

The image of Jesus as a man of prayer emerges again at the end of his life. *Jesus spends his last night in prayer to his Father in the Garden of Gethsemane* (22:39-46). While Matthew and Mark also have an account of Jesus' agony in the garden, Luke transforms this account into an example for his followers. The whole episode is included between two statements: at the beginning, Jesus says, "Pray that you may not undergo the test" (22:40); at the end he challenges them, "Get up and pray that you may not undergo the test" (22:46). Jesus prays with such intensity and agony that "his sweat became like drops of blood falling on the ground" (22:44). Jesus' example shows his disciples that they are to turn to God in prayer in times of testing. Their prayer must always be made according to God's will with the same confident assurance that God will be with them: "Father, if you are willing, take this cup away from me; still, *not my will but yours be done*" (22:42). This is a powerful example for the disciples to follow.

On the cross, Jesus prays for the final time to his Father. In contrast to the cry of desperation that utters from the mouth of Jesus in the gospels of Matthew and Mark, Luke's Jesus shows how he lives out his own teaching. He prays to the Father to forgive his enemies: "Father, forgive them, they know not what they do" (23:34). At the moment of death, Jesus entrusts himself in faith to his Father as he cries out, "Father, into your hands I commend my spirit" (23:46). Luke offers these prayers of Jesus as an example for his followers to show how Jesus' spirituality enables one to face opposition and death. Stephen, the first martyr, embraces Jesus' spirituality and prays in an identical way when he is being stoned to death (Acts 7:59-60).

Spirituality of Confident Trust in God

On the journey, Luke's Jesus invites his followers to a total dependence upon God (12:22-34). He instructs them to put aside all worry: "Therefore I tell you, do not worry about your life and what you will eat, or about your body and what you will wear" (12:22). They are to place their confidence in God's love and care for them. This trust is based upon God's providential caring love for the creation: "If God so clothes the grass in the field that grows today and is thrown into the oven tomorrow, will he not much more provide for you, O you of little faith?" (12:28).

Spirituality of Forgiveness and Repentance

The theme of forgiveness and repentance is evident as well in the spirituality of Jesus' journey. Chapter 15 contains three important parables that express Jesus' concern for those who are lost and the Father's unconditional forgiveness for those who have strayed.

The parable of the Lost Sheep (15:4-7) focuses on a shepherd's joy in finding the one sheep that went astray. Jesus makes the comparison that a similar joy will be experienced in heaven over the repentance of one lost sinner (15:7).

The parable of the Lost Coin (15:8-10) illustrates a widow's joy at finding her lost coin. Again, Jesus compares her joy to the joy heaven experiences at the repentance of a sinner (15:10).

The parable of the Prodigal Son (15:11-32) is one of the most well-known parables. Three characters appear in the story: the younger son, the older son, and the Father. A focus on each of these characters illustrates further dimensions of this spiritual theme of repentance and forgiveness. The younger son sets off on a journey diametrically different from the journey Jesus and his disciples have embraced. The younger son's journey is away from his father into "a life of dissipation" (15:13). Eventually he comes to his senses and returns to his father, requesting forgiveness: "Father, I have sinned against heaven and against you; I no longer deserve to be called your son" (15:21). His statement of repentance gives insight into the very nature of sin. The younger son acknowledges that the evil that he has committed has offended both God and his father. These two dimensions define sin itself: an offense against God and our fellow human being. Sin is never simply an offense against God—it always has a community dimension. The younger son realizes the consequences of his actions: "I no longer deserve to be called your son" (15:21). The response of the father in the parable is a perfect illustration of the response and reaction of God toward us sinners. Like the father in the story who is constantly on the lookout for the return of his son, God desperately desires the return of those sons and daughters who have gone astray. When they return, God welcomes them back with the same joy and happiness. This image is an example of total unconditional love. Like the father in the story, God accepts the sinner back fully and unconditionally.

Contrasted with the love, forgiveness, and generosity of the father is the third figure in the story, the older son. He is riddled with jealousy. He is jealous of the way his father has treated the younger son. His self-centeredness hinders him from entering into the joy and forgiveness of his father.

This parable is an incredible challenge for readers of every age to appropriate some important lessons for their spiritual journey. Honest, sincere repentance leads to the experience of God's unconditional love and forgiveness that restores us to full relationship with God as Father. Like

God, we are all called to share in God's love and joy at the repentance and forgiveness of others. We are called to turn from self-centeredness to a God-centered vision permeated by the unconditional virtues of love and forgiveness.

Spiritual Concern for the Poor and the Dangers of Wealth

In the account of Jesus' birth, Luke highlights a theme that becomes central to his whole spirituality: Jesus' identification with and concern for the poor. Jesus was born in a stable and placed "in a manger because there was no room for them in the inn" (2:7). In his birth, Jesus identifies with the homeless. The first to receive the message of Jesus' birth are poor shepherds living in the fields (2:8-14). Jesus' concern for the poor is reinforced in the Beatitudes (6:20-26), where Jesus proclaims a blessing on those who are *economically* poor: "Blessed are you who are poor, for the kingdom of God is yours" (6:20). In contrast, Matthew's gospel focuses upon *spiritual* poverty (Matt 5:3).

Luke's account of the Beatitudes is followed by a list of woes that further reflects a strong condemnation of the rich: "Woe to you who are rich, for you have received your consolation. But woe to you who are filled now, for you will be hungry" (6:24-25). In the course of his journey, Jesus directs attention to the evils perpetrated by wealth. Jesus sets forth a principle that explains his spiritual vision regarding wealth: "Take care to guard against all greed, for though one may be rich, one's life does not consist of possessions" (12:15). Jesus illustrates this principle with a parable about the "rich fool" intent on amassing more and more possessions (12:16-21). The futility of his greed is highlighted when he dies: "'You fool [says God], this night your life will be demanded of you; and the things you have prepared, to whom will they belong?'" (12:20-21). Jesus urges his followers to see wealth in its true perspective. Placed in the context of one's eternal destiny, wealth and possessions are just fleeting. One's ultimate concern should be one's relationship with God.

Jesus returns to his concern about the destructive power of possessions in the parable of the rich man and Lazarus (16:19-31). Not only does greed destroy one's relationship with God, as Jesus had noted above, but it also harms one's relationship with others, especially the poor. The contrast between the life of luxury led by the rich man and the destitution of Lazarus is striking. In his enjoyment of his wealth, the rich man remains oblivious to poor Lazarus laying outside his house. In the afterlife, their roles are reversed. One's life in the future kingdom of God depends upon how one has shown concern for the needs of our fellow brothers and sisters.

In his treatment of wealth and possessions, Jesus promotes a spirituality with the great commandment at its foundation: love of God and love of neighbor. Wealth has the power to turn one away from the very essence of being a follower of Jesus: a desire to love God and to remain in relationship with God. Greed replaces this desire with an all-consuming urge to amass more wealth. A follower of Jesus should be aware of and open to respond to the needs of others. Greed blinds us to the needs and situations of those around us. We are selfishly aware only of ourselves. This spiritual vision remains significant for every follower at every place and time.

Spirituality of Hospitality

Hospitality was the most sacred obligation throughout the ancient world. In the Old Testament, we recall stories such as that of Abraham who sees three men standing near his tent. Abraham immediately runs to greet them and invites them to rest with him while a meal is prepared (Gen 18:1-5). The sacred obligation of offering hospitality stems from their belief that God may be approaching in disguise. This is clearly the case in this passage: "The LORD appeared to Abraham by the terebinth of Mamre, as he sat in the entrance of his tent" (Gen 18:1). The same insight was held by the peoples of Greece and Rome. The well-known epic *Odyssey* narrates countless occasions on which Odysseus is accepted into people's homes due to his appeal to the sacred obligation of hospitality.

Against this background, many references to hospitality occur during Jesus' travel journey. On the road, moving from place to place, Jesus and his followers are dependent upon offers of hospitality. The Pharisees and scribes complain against Jesus because he was willing to receive hospitality from anyone: "This man welcomes sinners and eats with them" (15:2). This dispute reveals that the Pharisees have restricted the offer of hospitality! Jesus responds by showing through the subsequent parables that he extends a welcome to all who come his way—he does not exclude anyone from hospitality because of their religious or ethnic background. For Jesus, there are no boundaries to his gift of salvation.

Hospitality occurs largely in the context of a meal. Very often hospitality is an expression of Jesus' solidarity with the poor. Again on the journey Jesus speaks to the obligation of showing hospitality especially to the poor: "When you hold a banquet, invite the poor, the crippled, the lame, the blind; blessed indeed will you be because of their inability to repay you. For you will be repaid at the resurrection of the righteous" (14:13-14). Jesus teaches his followers that hospitality knows no limits, no boundaries. It should be extended to all according to need. Jesus shares meals with those who are sinners, tax collectors, women, men, Greeks, and Jews. All distinctions that humans make to separate peoples are ignored by Jesus. Following Jesus' example, hospitality truly is a sacred obligation to be expressed fully and all inclusively.

Luke's Spirituality Today

The spirituality that emerges from Luke's account of Jesus' life, death, and resurrection is a spirituality relevant for all periods, especially for the world of the twenty-first century. Ours is a world that is moving toward a closer connectedness with all peoples and recognizes our common humanity and our responsibility for the world we inhabit. The universal significance of Jesus as the one in whom the God of salvation is encountered is truly meaningful. The understanding of salvation as a deliverance from every form of evil gives hope to all people.

As Jesus was present to his disciples, instructing them and supporting them during their journey to Jerusalem, so Jesus continues to be present to us on our own journeys. His presence is felt especially through the power of God's Spirit. Throughout his two-volume work, Luke-Acts, God's Spirit guides and empowers people. Jesus was conceived through the power of the Spirit (1:35); John the Baptist identifies Jesus as the one who "will baptize you with the holy Spirit and fire" (3:16). Jesus begins his public ministry under the influence of God's Spirit: at his baptism the Holy Spirit came down upon him while he was praying (3:22); the Spirit then led him into the wilderness where he was tempted and God's Spirit was with him throughout his temptations (4:1). Jesus' entire ministry was under the power of God's Spirit: "Jesus returned to Galilee in the power of the Spirit, and news of him spread throughout the whole region" (4:14). At the beginning of the Acts of the Apostles, the Holy Spirit comes down upon the apostles gathered in prayer, fulfilling Jesus' promise that they would receive the gift of the Holy Spirit (Acts 1:8) to empower them to witness to Jesus' message. In the course of our own journey of faith, Jesus continues to be present to us through his Spirit communicating God's gift of salvation to us.

The world of North America and Europe today is characterized as *individualistic*. This individualism needs to be balanced with an awareness of and need for the *experience of community.* The spirituality of the Gospel of Luke does exactly this. Luke reminds us that in prayer we do not pray alone. We pray as members of a community, the church. Every petition of the Lord's prayer bears the stamp of praying together with and on behalf of others. We not only pray for our own sustenance but also for the sustenance of all: "Give us each day our daily bread" (11:3).

As Luke's spirituality is founded upon love, so today's spirituality needs the foundation of love to generate an authentic Christian spirituality. The parable of the Good Samaritan (10:29-37) challenges every believer to realize that love knows no boundaries—everyone is my neighbor. As such everyone deserves my love and respect. At the same time, Luke balances a spirituality that is solely focused on social action with one that needs to be rooted upon and inspired by an intimate encounter with God, as the story of Martha and Mary demonstrated (10:38-42).

An important aspect of Luke's spirituality for today is Jesus' spiritual instruction regarding the dangers of wealth. While there is so much wealth in our society, so many people are without the basic resources to lead a decent life. In summing up his whole teaching on wealth, Jesus offers an insightful challenge for all believers today: "Take care to guard against all greed, for though one may be rich, one's life does not consist of possessions" (12:15). In a consumer society that promotes a constant drive to acquire the most recent products available, it is worth being reminded that my life is not defined by what I have, but rather by my relationship to God and to one another. The parable of the rich man and Lazarus (16:19-31) challenges Christians today to open their eyes to the needs of the poor around them and to respond accordingly.

As the Gospel of Luke guided the spiritual lives of those early third-generation Christians, so this gospel continues to inspire and guide the spiritual lives of Christians today. When Luke quotes Jesus' first prophecy about his death from Mark's gospel, Jesus says, "If anyone wishes to come after me, he must deny himself and take up his cross *daily* and follow me" (9:23). Noteworthy is Luke's addition of the word "daily" to this saying. For Mark, this saying implied the imminent suffering and death of a follower of Jesus. Mark's readers at the beginning of the eighth decade of the first century were faced with the real possibility of suffering and death. The physical cross was very real for them. For Luke, the addition of the word *daily* shows that persecution has receded and the cross has now come to represent the acceptance of all the struggles and hardships believers face in the course of their daily lives. The same is true for believers in our own world. We are challenged to bear our own crosses, struggles, defeats, and disappointments each day of our faith journey. Stephen Barton calls this "a spirituality of the long haul."[3]

The spirituality emerging from the pages of the Gospel of Luke provides believers today with guidance and direction for living their lives in relationship with God and with one another. Luke's *journey spirituality* equips believers to respond unconditionally to Jesus as the universal Savior and to embrace a responsibility for every person as their neighbor.

CHAPTER FIVE

Exploring John's Spiritual Vision

The Gospel of John (also known as "the Fourth Gospel") is very different from the Synoptic Gospels (Matthew, Mark, and Luke). John's traditions handed on the good news from Jesus independently of the Synoptic Gospels. In art, John's gospel is often symbolized by the picture of an eagle. As an eagle soars through the sky and hovers over the earth, so this gospel appears to meditate and reflect upon Jesus, the Son of God, by drawing out the meaning and significance of Jesus in relation to the Father and to us. Some striking differences between John's gospel and the Synoptics are the following: John's gospel has no account of Jesus' birth. Instead, the gospel opens with a beautiful hymn that reflects upon the "Word" (1:1) and his relationship to the Father. The Son of God became man (1:14) to make the Father known to us ("No one has ever seen God. The only Son, God, who is at the Father's side, has revealed him" [1:18]) to enable us to "become children of God" (1:12). John has no account of the institution of the Eucharist at the Last Supper (as do Matt 26:26-30; Mark 14:22-26; and Luke 22:14-20). Instead, John reflects on the miracle of the multiplication of bread (6:1-15) as a sign of the gift of Jesus' body for his disciples (6:22-71): "I am the living bread that came down from heaven; whoever eats this bread will live forever; and the bread that I will give is my flesh for the life of the world" (6:51).

John expresses the gospel's purpose at the end of chapter 20: "But these are written that you may [come to] believe that Jesus is the Messiah, the Son of God, and that through this belief you may have life in his name" (20:31). These words, addressed to every reader of the gospel, show the writer's intention of bringing the readers to a deeper faith relationship with the person of Jesus, the Son of God.

The gospel's contents divide into two parts: *The Book of Signs* (chaps. 1–12), where seven signs (or miracles) lie at the heart of Jesus' ministry.

Jesus reveals himself to his disciples as the one who has come to replace Israel's traditions. The second part, *The Book of Glory* (chaps. 13–21), presents Jesus' Last Supper with his disciples in the context of his farewell discourses before it narrates the account of his death, resurrection, and appearances to his followers. From the earliest times of the Christian church, the Gospel of John has been termed the "Spiritual Gospel" because it reflects on the person of Jesus and his significance for us "children of God."[1]

Encountering God as Father in Jesus, the Son

A Personal Spirituality

A unique personal bond exists between Jesus, the Son, and the Father. God's revelation comes in the *person* of God's Son made *incarnate* among us. The beautiful hymn that serves as prologue to the gospel expresses well this personal relationship. Jesus is "the Word [who] became flesh and made his dwelling among us, and we saw his glory, the glory as of the Father's only Son, full of grace and truth" (1:14). In the New Testament, the reference to "the Word" (*logos* in Greek) is unique to the writings of John. This concept betrays a background in both the Greek and Hebrew traditions.[2] As the Word Incarnate, Jesus speaks God's word to humanity, making God, the Father, known in a uniquely intimate way. The personal bond between the Word and the Father effects the most complete revelation of God to humanity. The term "Word" (or *logos*) is aptly suited for communicating an understanding of God. The Word alone can make the Father known to humanity: "The only Son, God, who is at the Father's side, has revealed him" (1:18). With this term "Word," the prologue gives direction and purpose to the entire gospel. The Word, incarnated in the person of Jesus, makes the Father known. As the Word made flesh, Jesus teaches that he is the only way to the Father (14:6) and invites us into the closest personal relationship with God as God's children (1:12), who are promised the inheritance of eternal life (3:16).

Jesus' use of the phrase "I AM" throughout the gospel underscores this personal spirituality. God had revealed his name to Moses as "I AM" (Exod 3:14). The Israelites used this name for God throughout the Old Testament. In John's gospel, Jesus appropriates this term "I AM" for himself. This phrase is the clearest statement Jesus makes in John's gospel about his divinity. A good illustration of this occurs in the account of Jesus' arrest in the Garden of Gethsemane. Jesus asks the arresting soldiers, "'Whom are you looking for?' They answered him, 'Jesus the Nazorean.' He said to them, 'I AM' . . . When he said to them, 'I AM,' they turned away and fell to the ground" (18:4-6). By describing the group falling to the ground at the mention of the name "I AM," John implies that they are in the presence of the divine. The appropriate response for anyone in the presence of divinity was to fall to the ground in worship. John makes very clear that Jesus is speaking in the manner of God.

Jesus also uses the phrase "I am" in connection with a descriptive predicate to indicate more fully his divinity: "*I am the bread of life*; whoever comes to me will never hunger, and whoever believes in me will never thirst" (6:35).[3] Jesus alone is the one who can fulfill everyone's longing for life by sustaining them forever. Jesus is also challenging his hearers/readers to make a decision for or against him. No one can remain indecisive.

Community Dimension

While the Gospel of John strongly emphasizes the personal bonds between the Father and the Son, it also embraces a very strong community dimension within God. The Father and the Son are spoken of as one. In response to Philip, Jesus says, "Do you not believe that I am in the Father and the Father is in me?" (14:10-11). The Spirit is also intimately associated with the Father and the Son: "the Spirit of truth . . . will glorify me, because he will take from what is mine and declare it to you" (16:13, 14). A unique, personal, intimate relationship exists between the Father, the Son, and the Spirit.

The believer enters into this community. In calling believers "children of God," John defines their essence and unique relationship to God. The prologue shows this relationship is a result of the Word becoming man: "But to those who did accept him he gave power to become children of God, to those who believe in his name, who were born not by natural generation nor by human choice nor by a man's decision but of God" (1:12-13). In Jesus' discussion with Nicodemus, Jesus takes up this theme by stressing the need to be "born from above" (3:3) to enter God's kingdom and so enter into relationship with God. Since the Greek word *anōthen* is ambiguous and means both "from above" and "again," Nicodemus misunderstands this phrase "born from above" as "born again" and rejects Jesus' words. Jesus replies to him, "No one can enter the kingdom of God without being born of water and Spirit. What is born of flesh is flesh and what is born of spirit is spirit" (3:5-6). The believer is born spiritually from above and enters into a deep spiritual relationship with God.

Spiritual Response to Jesus as the Word Incarnate, the Son of God

As "the human face of God,"[4] Jesus, the Word Incarnate, the Son of God, is the fullest representation for us humans of God. As believers, we are God's children. We discover our identity by reflecting on Jesus, the Son of God. He is the fulfillment of our most fundamental desires, such as our need for nourishment ("I am the bread of life" [6:35]), for the fullness of life ("I am the resurrection and the life" [11:25]), and for the discovery of the path to happiness ("I am the way and the truth and the life" [14:6]). How do we as humans respond to his offer to fulfill our essential human longings? An answer emerges from a consideration of the spirituality of two important dimensions in the gospel: Jesus' spiritual insights in the farewell discourses and the spirituality of personal encounters with Jesus.

Spirituality of the Farewell Discourses

Chapters 13–17 contain what scholars call "Jesus' farewell discourses." John opens this second part of his gospel with a clear identification of its central theme—Jesus' return to the Father: "Before the feast of Passover, Jesus knew that his hour had come to pass from this world to the Father" (13:1). For John, the culmination of Jesus' life and ministry is his return to the Father. The gospel narrative is situated between two points: the Word coming down from the Father (1:1-18) and the final return to the Father symbolized in the scene of Jesus' death: "When Jesus had taken the wine, he said, 'It is finished.' And bowing his head, he handed over the spirit" (19:30). In his final words, Jesus declares that he has completed the work the Father had given him to perform. In breathing his last breath, Jesus hands over his spirit and returns to the Father.

Washing of the Disciples' Feet (13:1-7)

The Last Supper is the context for the farewell discourses (13:1–17:26). John's narration of the Last Supper differs remarkably from the Synoptic account. The most striking difference is the absence of any account of the institution of the Eucharist in John's gospel. John had already reflected on the significance of the Eucharist after narrating the sign of the multiplication of bread (chap. 6). In place of the account of the institution of the Eucharist in the last discourses, John introduced the symbolic account of the footwashing. Jesus takes up a towel and a bowl of water to wash his disciples' feet. Peter is shocked by Jesus' act of humiliation (13:6-8). After washing his disciples' feet, Jesus explains its symbolism as an act of service and of humility. If their master, Jesus, is willing to wash his disciples' feet, they in turn must be willing to wash one another's feet: "I have given you a model to follow, so that as I have done for you, you should also do" (13:15). In a symbolic way, Jesus is calling on his followers to imitate his action by performing acts of service for others.

Further symbolism is evident in this episode. The footwashing becomes an acted out prophecy that Jesus is about to be humiliated further by his death. When Jesus responds to Peter's refusal to allow Jesus to wash his feet, Jesus replies, "Unless I wash you, you will have no inheritance with me" (13:8). Since sharing in Jesus' "inheritance" (his gift of eternal life) can only come through his death by which he attains our salvation, the footwashing is symbolic for Jesus' death. Added to this, the footwashing is also symbolic for baptism, as Jesus implies when he says to Peter, "Whoever has *bathed* has no need except to have his feet washed, for he is clean all over" (13:10). The New Testament sometimes uses the Greek word *louein*, "to wash or bathe," in a cultic way to refer to "baptism" (see 1 Cor 6:11 and Titus 3:5).[5] In 13:10 Jesus is saying that if one has already been baptized, then there is no need to be baptized again. The footwashing symbolizes baptism by which the effects of Jesus' death are communicated to the believer.

Two important aspects emerge for the believer's spirituality. Jesus' symbolic action of humiliation shows that every believer is called to a life of service. This episode also indicates that his death made possible the relationship between the believer and Jesus. In a symbolic way, Jesus has set forth two central aspects for the lives of every believer: a relationship with God (through baptism) and service of others. Here we see again the human face of God in the actions of Jesus. Like every Christian believer since the beginning of the gospel narrative, we are challenged today to embrace the spiritual relationship with Jesus that we received in our baptism. We should also be ready to serve the needs of our brothers and sisters.

Spirituality Founded on Love (13:31-35)

Following the account of the footwashing, Jesus tells his disciples that he "will be with you only a little while longer" (13:33). Jesus offers his followers advice to guide them when he is no longer with them. The central spiritual message Jesus leaves his disciples is his instruction on the *new commandment of love*: "I give you a new commandment: love one another. As I have loved you, so you also should love one another" (13:34). The newness of this commandment lies not in the content, since it is already found in Leviticus 19:18, but in the imitation of Jesus' love for us: "As I have loved you, so you also should love one another" (13:34).

A spirituality centered on love directs every believer's life. Love begins with the love that God has for humanity, a love God demonstrated by sending his Son into the world (3:16). Love unites the Father, the Son, and the disciples. This love is communicated from the Father through the Son to all believers, who in turn share it with each other. The Father loves the Son because he is willing to lay down his life for others: "This is why the Father loves me, because I lay down my life in order to take it up again" (10:17). The Son demonstrates his love for the Father through his obedience: "But the world must know that I love the Father and that I do just as the Father has commanded me" (14:31). The Father loves the believer just as he loves the Son (17:23).

John's gospel contains very little ethics. The only law Jesus gives his disciples is the law of love: "This is my commandment: love one another as I love you" (15:12). While the Synoptic Gospels express the great commandment as a command to love one's neighbor as one's self, John's gospel models the command to love in the way Jesus has loved them. Believers are challenged to imitate Jesus' love: "No one has greater love than this, to lay down one's life for one's friends. You are my friends if you do what I command you" (15:13-14). Their love demonstrates the closeness of their relationship with Jesus. Love bears witness to the essential bond of love between all believers: "This is how all will know that you are my disciples, if you have love for one another" (13:35).

Without doubt John's spirituality is timeless. While John situates the Jesus of the farewell discourses in the Upper Room on the night before his death, it is as though Jesus is addressing a message from heaven to believers of every age. Spirituality centered on love is the foundation for every believer's life. A spirituality of love unites us to the Father and Son and is further expressed in a love that moves outwards toward others. Love is open to everyone.

Spirituality of Eternal Life

"Do not let your hearts be troubled. You have faith in God; have faith also in me" (14:1). Although Jesus is about to leave his followers, he encourages their continued trust in him. The heart of his encouragement is contained in his saying, "I am the way and the truth and the life. No one comes to the Father except through me" (14:6). This saying reminds the reader of the purpose for which the gospel was written (20:31): believing in Jesus brings the *promise of eternal life*. The only way to attain this life is through faith in the Son (3:16). The prologue of the gospel opens with the statement that the Word brings life to all (1:4), the very life of God in which the Son shares (5:26). The Son became human so that he in turn could communicate this life to those who believe: "I came so that they might have life and have it more abundantly" (10:10).

God's life is communicated now and continues on into eternity: it is eternal life. Jesus offers a spirituality that focuses on the *present aspect of this life*, not on the future. Through faith in the Son we already possess the spiritual life of God. This is an awesome gift we have been given. This insight into eternal life gives guidance to our spirituality on how to live our lives in the present. This guidance is provided by the Jesus of the Gospel of John.

Spirituality Rooted in the Spirit

Of all the gospels, the Gospel of John reflects far more on the role of the Spirit in the life of the believer. When Jesus encounters the Jewish leader Nicodemus, he speaks of the necessity of being born from above by water and the Spirit: "Amen, amen, I say to you, no one can enter the kingdom of God without being born of water and Spirit. What is born of flesh is flesh and what is born of spirit is spirit" (3:5). The farewell discourses meditate more fully on the role the Spirit plays in the lives of believers (see 14:15-17; 14:26; 15:26-27; 16:4-11; 16:12-15). Jesus introduces a new term to refer to the Spirit, namely, *paraklētos* (often transliterated into English as *Paraclete* [or advocate, counselor, comforter]) that refers literally to someone who speaks "on behalf of another."[6] "The Spirit of truth" guides into the truth all who hear Jesus' instructions (16:13). The Spirit comes into the hearts of every believer and acts as a teacher helping them to understand Jesus' message more fully: "The Advocate, the holy Spirit that the Father will send in my name—he will teach you everything and remind you of all that [I] told you" (14:26). The Spirit remains true to Jesus' preaching. The Spirit does not communicate any new teaching but gives the believer insight into what Jesus had already taught. Jesus fulfills his promise of the gift of the Spirit at his resurrection: "He breathed on them and said to them, 'Receive the holy Spirit'" (20:22).

This reflection on the gift of the Spirit in the life of the believer shows that the Spirit is the foundation for the spiritual life of every believer. The Spirit dwells in the heart of every believer and gives insight into the relevance of Jesus' message for their lives. As a living teacher, the Spirit does not simply repeat a tradition from the past, but inspires believers to understand the relevance and importance of Jesus' teachings for their lives.

Spirituality of Mutual Indwelling

In the allegory of the vine and the branches (15:1-10), Jesus illustrates the importance of remaining united with him. As branches must remain united to the vine if they are to draw life-giving nourishment from the vine, so Jesus calls on his hearers to remain united to him if they are to draw true spiritual nourishment: "Remain in me, as I remain in you. Just as a branch cannot bear fruit on its own unless it remains on the vine, so neither can you unless you remain in me" (15:4).

In his final prayer to his Father, Jesus asks the Father that believers may be united to him and to the Father in a way analogous to the way the Son remains united to the Father: "I pray not only for them, but also for those who will believe in me through their word, so that they may all be one, as you Father, are in me and I in you, that they also may be in us, that the world may believe that you sent me" (17:20-21). Our spirituality draws life from our union with the Father and Son.

The spirituality of the final prayer of Jesus (17:1-26) gives insight into an understanding of the true effects of prayer: prayer unites the believer with the Father, the Son, and all fellow believers. Through prayer the Son makes known that he has come to dwell within the believer in love. As Raymond Brown expresses it, "Jesus draws all of us into his embrace. The world has refused to hear his Father; but we who believe have known the Father, and thus have a share in his love and in his Son."[7]

Summary

Like Matthew's Sermon on the Mount (5:1–7:29) and Luke's journey to Jerusalem (9:51–19:27), John's farewell discourses contain the heart of his spirituality. In the person of Jesus, we encounter the fullness of the divinity. Through Jesus' actions in the footwashing, the spiritual importance of service and love of others emerges. The Father, Son, and Spirit come to dwell in us and we in turn are brought into relationship with them. This unique spirituality brings an intimacy into the relationship between Jesus and those who believe in him. At the heart of John's spirituality is the gift of the Spirit that enables believers to gain insight into Jesus' message for the present. Sharing in the intimate life of the Father and Son means that we too must extend that love outside ourselves. With Jesus as our example for love, we are challenged to show a love that embraces everyone.

Spirituality of Personal Encounters with Jesus

Jesus' dialogues with many individuals lie at the heart of John's gospel. In each encounter, Jesus challenges the individual to enter into a spiritual relationship with him. In illustrating these encounters, John shows the level of their faith relationship. These encounters become examples by which we can reflect on our own faith relationship with Jesus and how to develop it more fully.

Nicodemus (3:1-15; 7:50-52; 10:39-42)

Nicodemus appears in three different scenes in the gospel. He is a Pharisee, a well-respected leader of the people of Israel and a member of the Jewish council, the Sanhedrin (3:1). He is conflicted. He respects Jesus and acknowledges that God is working through him: "Rabbi, we know that you are a teacher who has come from God, for no one can do these signs that you are doing unless God is with him" (3:2). At the same time, Nicodemus "came to Jesus at night" (3:2), showing his reluctance to be seen openly in Jesus' company out of fear for his fellow Israelites and the Jewish council.

In a later episode (7:50-52), Nicodemus comes to Jesus' defense by appealing to the law of Israel that gives people the right to state their case before being condemned. He tries to shield Jesus from harm. Nicodemus appears in a final scene with Joseph of Arimathea (19:39-42). They come together to bury the body of Jesus. Nicodemus had bought expensive spices to perform the ritual washing (19:39). *Nicodemus and Joseph symbolize those who have come to believe in Jesus but are not ready to confess their belief.* They are afraid of the reprisals they may suffer (19:38), such as exclusion from the synagogue (12:42). Theirs is a spirituality based upon an inadequate, limited faith.

Samaritan Woman (4:2-42)

Jesus' discourse with the Samaritan woman follows the discourse with Nicodemus. John contrasts the response of a Samaritan foreigner with an Israelite leader. The Samaritan woman's response was on a deeper level. When Jesus asks the Samaritan woman for a drink of water, he breaks two social rules—talking with a woman in public and associating with Samaritans. *Jesus shows that he meets people where they are in their spiritual journey, then leads them to a deeper spiritual level.* By requesting a drink of ordinary water, Jesus presents himself as the living water from above (4:13-14). He explains further that true religion is based not upon a place (like the temple of Jerusalem or the worship on Mount Gerizim), but on himself.

The Samaritan woman becomes a missionary in her own right. She returned home and proclaimed to her own people that she had found "the Messiah" (4:29). She exemplifies the true response in encountering Jesus: to go forth and proclaim that encounter to others. She calls her fellow Samaritans to come and see who this person is. They heed her call and come to Jesus. Many believed in him because of her word (4:39). The spirituality illustrated in the Samaritan woman's response shows that God embraces everyone who is open and sincere. There are no distinctions in our relationship with Jesus. An important aspect of John's gospel emerges here: the believer must bear witness to Jesus. John the Baptist was the first witness to Jesus; now a Samaritan woman witnesses to her encounter with Jesus among her own people.

Judas (12:1-8; 13:27)

John's portrayal of Judas differs from that of the Synoptic Gospels. John's perspective emerges from his side comments. In the story of the anointing at Bethany (12:1-8), Judas criticizes the woman for wasting her money on such frivolous items as this costly oil instead of supporting the poor. John comments that Judas was motivated not by a sincere concern for the poor, but "because he was a thief and held the money bag and used to steal the contributions" (12:6). Later, before Judas departs from the meal with Jesus and the other disciples, John comments that "Satan entered him" (13:27). On the spiritual level, *Judas represents the disciple who betrays Jesus.* He moves from being within Jesus' closest circle to the side of the evil one. The betrayal could not be any worse.

Thomas (20:24-30)

Thomas is another of Jesus' closest followers. He is a "realist more than (a) doubter."[8] Thomas was not with the other disciples when Jesus appeared to his disciples after being raised from the dead. He refused to believe: "Unless I see the mark of the nails in his hands and put my finger into the nail marks and put my hand into his side, I will not believe" (20:25). *Thomas represents those whose faith is based upon signs.* His spirituality rests upon material evidence rather than on faith in God's power. He eventually comes to believe and confesses Jesus as "My Lord and my God!" (20:28). Jesus pronounces a blessing on those who, unlike Thomas, "have not seen and have believed" (20:29). Our spirituality rests not on the evidence of seeing the risen Jesus (as Thomas had), but on the witness and testimony of others.

Beloved Disciple (13:23-25; 19:26-27; 19:35; 20:2-10; 21:7; 21:20-25)

The Beloved Disciple is a significant character in John's gospel. Beyond identifying him as "the disciple whom Jesus loved," the author never reveals who he is. Scholars today see him as a historical character who has taken on a representative role. *The Beloved Disciple represents the ideal disciple, the true believer.* The first reference to him is in the context of Jesus' Last Supper with his disciples. The narrator describes him in very graphic terms: "One of his disciples, the one whom Jesus loved, was reclining at Jesus' side" (13:23). The translators of the New American Bible have failed to capture the significance of this description both here and in 1:18. Literally, this verse (13:23) should read, "was reclining *on the bosom of Jesus* [*en tō kolpō tou Iēsou*]." This reminds the reader of the description of the relationship between Jesus and the Father in the prologue, which reads literally, "The only Son, God, who is *in the bosom of the Father* [*eis ton kolpon tou patros*]" (1:18). The meaning of the two phrases is the same in the Greek. The closeness of this disciple to Jesus is analogous to the closeness of Jesus to the Father. This explains why he is Jesus' closest disciple—his spiritual relationship with Jesus is equivalent to that of Jesus with his Father.

Another episode reveals the depth of this disciple's faith. He is present with the mother of Jesus at the foot of the cross (19:25-27). Of all the disciples, the Beloved Disciple has remained true and faithful to Jesus to the end. Before he dies, Jesus gives this disciple to his mother, and his mother in like manner to this disciple. Because of his faith and love, Jesus has accepted this disciple as part of his spiritual family. Through this episode Jesus stresses *symbolically* that all believers can become members of his spiritual family through faith and love.

The Beloved Disciple was the first to believe in Jesus' resurrection. When he entered the empty tomb, "he saw and believed" (20:8). In contrast, the narrator notes that Peter went into the tomb first and simply "saw." The Beloved Disciple was able to see with the eyes of faith because of the depth of his love for Jesus. He was also the first to recognize the risen Jesus at the Sea of Tiberias (21:7). His love enabled him to see with the eyes of faith what others could not see and to acknowledge that the risen Lord was present on the shore of Tiberias. A relationship of love is foundational for coming to faith in the risen Lord.

In the final episode of the gospel, the narrator returns to the importance of love in the relationship with the risen Lord. Jesus asks Peter three times about his love for him (21:15-19). The threefold question reverses Peter's threefold denial of Jesus (18:15-18, 25-27). Jesus implies that Peter needs to have the depth of love that the Beloved Disciple has—love is the unconditional requirement for a disciple.

The concluding verses of the gospel (21:24-25) point to another characteristic of this ideal disciple: he is a *witness*. He is the link in the chain between Jesus and this gospel that records his witness: "It is this disciple who *testifies* to these things and has written them, and we know that his *testimony* is true" (21:24). He has borne witness to everything that Jesus said and did. This gospel has been written from his testimony and provides the foundation for the faith of all who read it.

Through this presentation of the Beloved Disciple as the ideal disciple, John illustrates what the spirituality of a true follower of Jesus entails. The spiritual relationship between Jesus and his disciples is founded upon faith and *love*. Love brings the Beloved Disciple to *witness* to his experiences. His love drives him to share this love with others. Faith, love, witness—these are the cardinal virtues of the spiritual life.

John's Spirituality Today

John's spirituality starts with the Word of God becoming incarnate. It is a spirituality of God's initiative and the call for our response. "The Word became flesh" is the source of the fullness of God's grace (1:16-17). John's spirituality is founded upon the personal bond between Jesus, the Son of God, and his Father. His spirituality also calls for the realization that each of us is united to the person of Jesus in the manner in which branches are part of a vine. We all need to be individually united to the same vine, that is, Christ. The term "children of God" defines our common nature in regard to each other and to God. A spirituality of equality emerges in our interaction with one another and in our identity as "God's children." We all receive life by remaining attached to Jesus, the vine. When Jesus had completed his mission and returned to the Father, he did not leave us orphans but gave us another Paraclete, the Holy Spirit (16:5-15). John's reflection on the gift of the Spirit who will replace Jesus intimates that the Spirit is the foundation for the spiritual life of every believer.

In focusing on certain individual faith-responses to Jesus in his gospel, John presents different depths of spirituality. Each character was invited to enter into a personal relationship with Jesus through faith. Each one responded differently. *Judas* started in a spiritual relationship with Jesus but then turned away and betrayed him. *Nicodemus* represents those who are interested in a spiritual-faith relationship with Jesus, but are unable to commit openly because of the pressures around them. The *Samaritan woman*, by contrast, is gently led by Jesus to the realization that he truly answers her needs. The openness in her encounter with Jesus brings her to a deeply spiritual relationship that she immediately shares with her own people. *Thomas* is an example of the disciple who has placed his reliance on physical signs in his relationship with Jesus. However, through his encounter with the risen Jesus, he realizes his need for trust in the risen Lord. In contrast to Thomas, the risen Jesus blesses us because we have believed without seeing him. Ours is a spirituality that is founded on trust and the inspiration of the lives of former witnesses to the risen Jesus (20:29). The *Beloved Disciple* is the one person who demonstrates the most intimate spiritual relationship with Jesus, a relationship that is characterized by the qualities of faith, love, and witness. Since the Beloved Disciple is presented as the ideal disciple, we are called to be guided by these same qualities.

In these spiritual encounters, Jesus takes people where they are and leads them to a deeper level of intimacy with himself and the Father. For example, in the encounter with the Samaritan woman, Jesus never condemned her for the life she had led with five husbands (4:16-19). Instead, he meets her where she is and leads her to a deeper spiritual awareness of how she is to live her life. The same is true of Peter, who had denied Jesus three times. Jesus meets him where he is and challenges Peter to confess his love for him three times. In this way, Jesus restores Peter to a spiritual relationship with him.

These faith responses serve as paradigms for us on our spiritual journey today. We are called to embrace a spirituality that places Jesus at the center of our lives. We are called to enter into a relationship founded on faith and love. The gospel assures us that this relationship is one that grows and develops over time. We may begin at the level of a Nicodemus or a Thomas. If we respond to his grace, Jesus draws us always upward to a deeper level in our faith relationship with him until we embrace the depth of a relationship marked by faith and love.

At the same time, these individual relationships with Jesus need to be tempered with the imagery of the vine and the branches (15:1-7). In our relationship with Jesus we are united with others who are also in an intimate relationship with the risen Jesus. Together we are all united to the one vine, that is, Jesus.

At the heart of John's spirituality is love. Love is the foundation for the relationship among the Father and the Son and is extended to believers. We enter into this love relationship with God the Father and Son through belief. Instead of speaking to numerous ethical situations and providing many ethical laws, the Gospel of John stresses love as the foundation for all ethics. John's vision speaks directly to our twenty-first-century world. Many criticisms from young people about religion concern their perception that religion is legalistic. John's gospel clearly speaks to young people today by touching the heart of the Christian religion, namely, a living love relationship with God and with one another. Such love knows no limits.

PART TWO

Biblical Spirituality:
Incarnate and Alive

In a General Audience in January 2010, Pope Benedict XVI called on Christians to turn to the lives of the saints to discover the spiritual message of the Scriptures:

> Truly, dear friends, the saints are the best interpreters of the Bible. As they incarnate the word of God in their own lives, they make it more captivating than ever, so that it really speaks to us.[1]

The Scriptures are the foundation of our rich Catholic spiritual tradition. The following chapter will explore briefly how the Scriptures have served as the inspiration for making incarnate Jesus' spiritual vision. Most often events prompted Christians to turn to the Scriptures in prayer and contemplation for direction and for ways to respond. Every age has appropriated the Bible's spiritual vision in ways that make relevant this timeless spiritual message for a new age and period.

For each gospel, we offer two examples (one from the past, another from the recent present) of Christians who appropriated for themselves and for their times a specific spiritual vision. Their spirituality continues to endure long after their deaths as testimony to the ongoing relevance and lasting value of this evangelical spirituality.

CHAPTER SIX

Biblical Spirituality Incarnated

God's Transformative Presence with Us—
Matthew's Spirituality

The Gospel of Matthew is a source for many traditions within Catholic spirituality. Here I shall focus on one spiritual theme that has been enormously influential throughout the Christian centuries: the awareness of Christ's transformative presence with us. In chapter 2, I showed that Matthew's spiritual vision was inspired by God's presence in Jesus (1:23) and Christ's promise that he would be present with his disciples "until the end of the age" (28:20).

The two examples that I shall explore (one a canonized saint, Antony, from the early Christian church; the other not yet canonized, Dorothy Day, from more recent times) illustrate how they encountered this transformative presence of Christ in similar, yet very distinctive, ways.

St. Antony (250–356)

Antony is considered the "Father of Monasticism." Although Christian hermits lived alone before his time, Antony's life influenced the spread of an authentic monasticism within the spiritual traditions of the church. The source for our knowledge of Antony comes chiefly from a work, *The Life of St. Antony*, written by St. Athanasius of Alexandria between 356 and 362. Athanasius wrote this biography in response to requests from monks "in foreign parts"[1] who wanted to learn about Antony's way of life and teachings in order to imitate him.

The ascetical teaching of the gospels, especially the Gospel of Matthew, fascinated and inspired Antony. This teaching drove him to adopt an austere way of life. Webster's Dictionary defines ascetical as "a person who practices self-denial and self-mortification for religious reasons . . . a person who leads an austerely simple, nonmaterialist life."[2] Antony's life truly epitomizes this definition.

Antony's parents were wealthy Egyptian Catholics who instilled in him a love of the Christian faith. His parents died when he was around eighteen. Six months later, while walking to church, Antony was reflecting on "how the Apostles left everything and followed the Savior; also how the people in Acts sold what they had and laid it at the feet of the Apostles for distribution among the needy, and what great hope is laid up in Heaven for them."[3] On entering the church, Antony heard the passage (from the Gospel of Matthew) being read where the rich young man asked Jesus, "Teacher, what good must I do to gain eternal life?" (19:16-22). Looking into this young man's heart, Jesus identifies what hinders him from following him: "If you wish to be perfect, go, sell what you have and give to [the] poor, and you will have treasure in heaven. Then come, follow me" (19:21). Antony believed these words were directed to him. He also sold whatever he possessed and gave the money to the poor. He kept back some money for the care of his sister.

On another occasion in church, he heard the words from Matthew's Sermon on the Mount, "Therefore, I tell you, do not worry about your life, what you will eat [or drink], or about your body, what you will wear. Is not life more than food and the body more than clothing?" (6:25-34). Again Antony took this text personally and responded immediately. He went to live a short distance outside his village where he devoted himself to an austere ascetical life. He had no material possessions and devoted his life to prayer in the spirit of Jesus' teaching in Matthew's gospel: "When you pray, do not be like the hypocrites, who love to stand and pray in the synagogues and on street corners so that others may see them. . . . But when you pray, go to your inner room, close the door, and pray to your Father in secret" (6:5-6).

Antony worked to support himself, relying on the admonition of St. Paul "that if anyone was unwilling to work, neither should that one eat" (2 Thess 3:10). After supplying his own needs from his earnings, Antony gave the rest to the poor. In this way, Antony anticipated the Rule of St. Benedict, the "Father of Western Monasticism," that instructed monks "to pray and to work" (*ora et labora*). Athanasius narrates many more events in the life of Antony. This brief summary has intended to capture the essence of Antony's ascetical life.

St. Antony's Spirituality for Today

Antony's austere life was not an end in itself, but a means to find and experience God's presence. Through prayer, fasting, and work (the ascetical life), Antony encountered God's transformative presence. He lived a long and holy life. Athanasius sums up Antony's influence in this way: "For Antony gained renown not for his writings, nor for worldly wisdom, nor for any art, but solely for his service of God. And that this was something God-given no one could deny."[4] Antony's spirituality was inspired by the Scriptures. His ascetical life rested especially on Jesus' teaching in Matthew's gospel. Prayer, solitude, fasting, almsgiving were the center of his life. These same practices remain at the heart of monastic spirituality today. While not all Christians are called to embrace such an austere life as Antony did, his appropriation of these biblical spiritual values of prayer, fasting, solitude, and almsgiving draws attention to their importance for the spiritual life of all Christians. They are a valuable means for encountering God's presence. Without doubt they are the central spiritual pillars that support and energize Christian spirituality.

Dorothy Day (1897–1980)

Dorothy Day, founder of the Catholic Worker Movement, also experienced the transformative presence of God in her life. Her discovery did not take place in the desert, as with Antony, but in the world itself, in the lives of the poor. Dorothy was also inspired by the ascetical spirituality of Matthew's Jesus. In fact, Dorothy's life expressed the second part of Webster's definition on asceticism mentioned above, namely, "a person who leads an austerely simple, nonmaterialist life."[5] While Antony's ascetical spirituality embraced a life of contemplation, prayer, and isolation, Dorothy's inspired a life of social action, justice, and a striving for peace. Two things gave her life meaning and direction: a concern for social justice and the importance of her religious faith.

Dorothy's awareness of the inequalities and injustices within society arose early in life. While studying in 1914 at the University of Illinois, she spent most of her time reading in the area of radical socialism. This period in her life sparked a lifelong concern for the poor and the "social evils" in the world.[6] At college, Dorothy identified with the poor. She supported herself, refusing any financial help from her father. After two years, she left college to start work in New York as a journalist for a socialist daily newspaper, *The Call*. Dorothy discovered firsthand the injustices of the social order. This concern remained with her throughout her life. She never embraced any political party, preferring her independence in order to maintain the ability to see social issues in an unbiased way.

In her early years, Dorothy did not have any religious convictions. The influence of others and of events themselves brought her slowly to embrace the Catholic Church. In her autobiography, Dorothy speaks of how from time to time she became aware of the spirituality of Catholicism. Two experiences are worth noting as they illustrate her developing spirituality, her awareness of God's transforming presence, and the power of the witness of one's life. She recalls an incident as a youngster when she went to a friend's house to play:

> Thinking the children must be in the front room, I burst in and ran through the bedrooms.
>
> In the front bedroom Mrs. Barrett was down on her knees, saying her prayers. She turned to tell me that Kathryn and the children had all gone to the store and then went on with her praying.[7]

This impression of the value of prayer in a person's life inspired Dorothy throughout her life. As a reporter in Chicago in her twenties, Dorothy shared accommodation with three women her own age. The spiritual dimensions of their lives intrigued her: their kindness toward her, their faithful attendance at Mass on Sundays and Holy Days, and the time they devoted to daily personal prayer "convinced me that worship, adoration, thanksgiving, supplication—these were the noblest acts of which men were capable in this life."[8]

In March 1927, Dorothy gave birth to her only child, Tamar Teresa Day. Her partner did not want children and their four-year relationship ended. In thanksgiving for the gift of her child, Dorothy had Tamar baptized in the Catholic Church:

> But I felt that only faith in Christ could give the answer. The Sermon on the Mount answered all the questions as to how to love God and one's brother. I knew little about the Sacraments, and yet here I was believing, knowing that without them Tamar would not be a Catholic.[9]

On December 28, 1927, Dorothy herself was received into the Catholic Church. Her spirituality flourished. Energized by Jesus' Sermon on the Mount, Dorothy's conversion also brought with it an ever-present awareness of God's guiding presence transforming her life. Some years later, in 1932, while covering a hunger march for *Commonweal* and *America* (two Catholic journals) in Washington, DC, she went to the

Shrine of the Immaculate Conception on the feast of the Immaculate Conception: "There I offered up a special prayer, a prayer which came with tears and with anguish, that some way would open up for me to use what talents I possessed for my fellow workers, for the poor."[10]

The next day her prayers were answered when she met Peter Maurin, a Frenchman, twenty years her senior. Maurin had embraced the Franciscan spirituality of poverty. He believed in a new society where gospel values would influence the lives of all within society. At his urging, Dorothy started a paper, *The Catholic Worker*, to promote the social teaching of the Catholic Church. The first publication in May 1933 comprised 2,500 copies. By December its circulation had risen to 100,000 copies!

In the paper, Maurin appealed for a renewal of the ancient practice of hospitality. Soon people were coming to Dorothy's apartment seeking a place to stay and something to eat. She responded to everyone in need regardless of their religious affiliation. She herself had little resources, but she remained true to her spirituality of trust in God.

The movement spread. In 1936, Dorothy's community moved into two buildings in Chinatown, New York, but still could not cope with those in need during this time of the Great Depression. The movement grew throughout the United States and within a few years thirty-three houses of hospitality run by the Catholic Worker had been opened. Dorothy spoke of the image of Jesus' outreach to the poor that gave direction to her whole spirituality:

> And (Jesus) directed His sublime words to the poorest of the poor, to the people who thronged the towns and followed after John the Baptist, who hung around, sick and poverty-stricken at the doors of rich men.
>
> He had set us an example and the poor and destitute were the ones we wished to reach.[11]

Following the spirituality of Jesus' teachings in Matthew's gospel, they cared for all whom they encountered. Jesus' words in the final parable of Matthew's gospel are exemplified in the life and attitude of Dorothy and the Catholic Worker Movement: "Come, you who are blessed by my Father. Inherit the kingdom prepared for you from the foundation of the world. For I was hungry and you gave me food" (25:31-46).

Dorothy Day's Spirituality for Today

This brief exploration of Dorothy's life and spirituality demonstrates how her trust in God and her desire to help those most in need in society animated her. From the beginning of the Catholic Worker Movement in 1933 until her death in 1980, Dorothy embraced an ascetical spirituality. She gave away everything she received to those who were poor. She did not discriminate between Catholics and those who were not. In her eyes, all people were made in God's image and deserved help and service, as Jesus showed in Matthew's parable quoted above. Prayer was the foundation for all she did. Through prayer and contemplation, she placed confidence in God's providence and guidance, reflecting again the spirit of the gospel: "Therefore I tell you, do not worry about your life, what you will eat [or drink], or about your body, what you will wear" (6:25).

Dorothy's spirituality provides us with a wonderful challenge today. Our times have changed, but her spirituality still remains relevant. In our contemporary society, so many people are hurting and suffering, lonely and afraid; Dorothy's spirituality invites us to be aware of their needs and to respond wherever we can. Her simple life is one we can strive to imitate: trust in God and care for one another. These are the ways we live out Jesus' commandment of loving God and loving our neighbor as ourselves. Hers is not simply a spirituality of action, but of action inspired by the Scriptures, especially the Gospel of Matthew and her consciousness of God's ever present providence and guidance.

In our consumer-orientated society with the ever present pressure and desire to acquire more and more material possessions, the spirituality of St. Antony and Dorothy Day is very relevant. Happiness and satisfaction are not attained in the quantity of possessions, but in a life of simplicity directed by the awareness of God's guiding presence and a concern for helping others. While there are many other dimensions to the spirituality of both St. Antony and Dorothy Day, the experience of the transformative presence of God in their lives was central to both. Antony experienced God's presence through an ascetical spirituality that withdrew him from the world where prayer and meditation were central. Dorothy's experience of God's presence led her to embrace an ascetical spirituality that was at home in the world. She dedicated her life to serve the poor and to rely upon God's grace and support in meeting their needs.

Following St. Antony, the monastic ascetical tradition has endured for some 1,700 years with monks remaining true to Antony's spirit. Following Dorothy Day, ordinary laypeople also strive to embrace her spirituality centered on hospitality and concern for the needs of the poor. The Catholic Worker Movement continues today with 185 communities worldwide and 168 communities in 37 states in the United States. Like

St. Antony who inspired the spirituality of monasticism, Dorothy Day inspired a spirituality whose very core embraced meeting the needs of the poor. A significant lesson she teaches us today is that social action always needs to be inspired and energized by the vision and teachings of the Scriptures. In her lifetime, many regarded Dorothy Day as a saint. Her famous response to such a statement was, "Don't call me a saint. I don't want to be dismissed so easily!" Nevertheless, her cause for canonization has been introduced as her spirituality truly embodies Jesus' values of caring for the needs of our human brothers and sisters in his name.

Martyrdom—Mark's Spirituality

One powerful theme emerged in our exploration of the spirituality of the Gospel of Mark—Jesus' suffering and death and its challenge for Jesus' followers: "Whoever wishes to come after me must deny himself, take up his cross, and follow me" (8:34). This demand has often been interpreted metaphorically as embracing our own struggles of daily Christian life as the Gospel of Luke interpreted it by inserting the word "daily": "If anyone wishes to come after me, he must deny himself and take up his cross *daily* and follow me" (Luke 9:23). However, Mark's gospel understood this challenge literally as following Jesus on the path to suffering and death. Mark's spirituality is indeed a spirituality for martyrs. The spiritual reality of following Jesus to death is rich in the history of Christianity. The Christian church has always flourished spiritually through the blood of martyrs. Here we will explore briefly the witness of three martyrs, two ancient and one recent: Sts. Perpetua and Felicity, and Archbishop Oscar Romero.

Sts. Perpetua and Felicity (died 203)

The early Christian church saw many Christians willingly embrace martyrdom. In most cases, they are remembered through legends surrounding their lives and deaths. However, an ancient text has survived, *The Passion of the Holy Martyrs Perpetua and Felicity*,[12] that was compiled from accounts written by Perpetua herself, her teacher Saturus, and others who had heard of their martyrdom.

Emperor Septimus Severus (193–211) continued the long-standing policy within the Roman Empire of not intentionally seeking out Christians for persecution. If someone was accused of being a Christian, they would be arrested and ordered to burn incense to the Roman emperor.

Should they refuse, they would be executed. Such had been the case with St. Polycarp of Smyrna (died 156). Septimus Severus, however, went further and outlawed conversion to Christianity because he was intent on strengthening his power by promoting religious syncretism.

In 203 in Carthage, Vibia Perpetua, from a well-educated and highly respected family, decided to become a catechumen, fully conscious of the consequences of her decision. One of her brothers followed her example. She was twenty-two years old, a widow, with a baby son still nursing at her breast. She was arrested together with four other catechumens, among them two slaves, Felicity and Revocatus. Before being brought to prison, Perpetua's father pleaded with her to change her mind. Perpetua recorded their conversation in her own words:

> "Father," said I, "do you see, let us say, this vessel lying here to be a little pitcher, or something else?" And he said, "I see it to be so." And I replied to him, "Can it be called by any other name than what it is?" And he said, "No." "Neither can I call myself anything else than what I am, a Christian."[13]

Perpetua and the others were baptized and received the gift of the Spirit, which strengthened them to face their impending martyrdom, as Perpetua wrote, "nothing else was to be sought for than bodily endurance."[14] She entrusted her infant son to her parents. Her separation from her child added to her suffering. During her imprisonment, Perpetua had three visions that strengthened her conviction that she would triumph through God's power.

The slave, Felicity, was already eight months pregnant. Roman law did not allow pregnant women to be put to death. Felicity was afraid that she would not give birth before the day set for their deaths and that Perpetua and the others would die and precede her to the heavenly kingdom. Two days before the execution, Felicity went into labor and gave birth to a baby girl who was adopted by a Christian woman of Carthage.

Perpetua's diary ends the day before their deaths. An eyewitness continues the account. The new Christians together with their catechist Saturus were brought into the amphitheater. There they faced the wild animals. Perpetua was the first to be thrown down. When she got up, she saw Felicity lying face down on the ground. She reached down and helped her up. Saturus was thrown to a leopard that bit him so badly that he was covered in blood. The Christians saw this as his second baptism and evidence of his salvation. They shouted out, "Washed and saved; washed and saved!" All the martyrs were brought to the center of the amphitheater. They kissed each other before their throats were slit. The writer concludes the account:

> But Perpetua, that she might taste some pain, being pierced be-
> tween the ribs, cried out loudly, and she herself placed the waver-
> ing right hand of the youthful gladiator to her throat. Possibly such
> a woman could not have been slain unless she herself had willed it,
> because she was feared by the impure spirit.
>
> O most brave and blessed martyrs! O truly called and chosen
> unto the glory of our Lord Jesus Christ![15]

Perpetua and Felicity's Spiritual Witness for Today

Over the centuries, many followers of Jesus have embraced martyrdom. This story of Perpetua and Felicity celebrates their acceptance
of martyrdom in imitation of Jesus. Although this account does not
expressly refer to the Gospel of Mark, it undoubtedly gives expression
to Mark's spirituality of martyrdom. On the first prediction of his death,
Mark's Jesus instructs his followers that to be true followers they must
also follow him into death: "Whoever wishes to come after me must deny
himself, take up his cross, and follow me. For whoever wishes to save
his life will lose it, but whoever loses his life for my sake and that of the
gospel will save it" (8:34-35). The lives of Perpetua, Felicity, and their
companions graphically demonstrate their acceptance of martyrdom.
Before receiving baptism, they were aware that their decision would
result in death—yet they embraced it. Through death as martyrs, they
experienced a second baptism of blood that gave them entry into the
life of God: "Washed and saved; washed and saved!" Both Perpetua
and Felicity eagerly embraced their forthcoming deaths. Felicity impa-
tiently awaited the birth of her baby girl so that she could join her fellow
Christians in a common martyrdom. Perpetua guided the gladiator's
hand to her throat in her attempt to embrace speedily the new life that
awaited her.

Although Perpetua and Felicity were martyrs from the third century,
they still hold enormous relevance for us today. They urge us to value
the gift of faith that leads to baptism. So valuable is this precious gift
that one must be willing to stand strong despite criticism and persecution. The faith of these two women is all the more astounding given the
times in which they lived. They are a true testimony to the depth of two
women's faith that willingly accepted Christian martyrdom. They are
also testimony to the working of God's Spirit, empowering them to give

their lives in imitation of the Lord Jesus Christ. They embraced the cross in the spirit of Jesus' challenge to his disciples.

Archbishop Oscar Romero (1917–1980)

Oscar A. Romero, one of the great martyrs of the twentieth century, was born in a mountain town in El Salvador on August 15, 1917. He was ordained in Rome in 1942 after receiving a Licentiate in Sacred Theology at the Gregorian University. His hope was to attain a doctorate in ascetical theology, but he returned to El Salvador to serve his people first in a rural parish and then later as rector of the Inter-Diocesan Seminary for twenty-three years. In 1970, he was appointed auxiliary bishop for the Archdiocese of San Salvador. Seven years later, on February 22, 1977, he became archbishop of San Salvador. The government and the military were pleased by his appointment as most people considered him conservative. However, their views would soon change. El Salvador was on the brink of civil war. General Humberto Romero (no relation of the archbishop) had proclaimed himself president. This action caused much opposition. Any form of protest or criticism was met with brutal retaliation.

On March 12, 1977, a priest friend of Archbishop Romero, Fr. Rutilio Grande, SJ, was murdered together with an elderly man and a young boy. They had given the priest a ride to the rural church where he was to celebrate Mass. Archbishop Romero was greatly disturbed by this murder and immediately offered Mass in the house where the bodies had been brought. In what was one of the most controversial decisions he was to make, Archbishop Romero canceled all Sunday Masses throughout the country for the next Sunday. The only Mass was held on the steps of the cathedral, where more than 100,000 people attended. Archbishop Romero demanded that the government look into the murders, but nothing happened. He grew more and more concerned about the government's brutality toward ordinary citizens. In a homily at the end of 1977 he said:

> Who knows if the one whose hands are bloodstained
> with Father Grande's murder,
> or the one who shot Father Navarro,
> if those who have killed, who have tortured,
> who have done so much evil, are listening to me?
> Listen, there in your criminal hideout,
> perhaps already repentant,
> you too are called to forgiveness.[16]

Every week for three years, Archbishop Romero broadcast his Sunday sermons on radio. He spoke out against conditions in the country and the horrendous murders and persecutions of ordinary citizens. People listened intently to these sermons in which he urged them to forgive and to work for a just and humane society. In his sermon of July 16, 1977, he said:

> Not just purgatory but hell awaits
> those who could have done good and did not do it.
> It is the reverse of the beatitude that the Bible has
> for those who are saved, for the saints,
> who could have done wrong and did not.
> Of those who are condemned it will be said:
> "They could have done good and did not."[17]

Altogether some 80,000 Salvadorans were to lose their lives in this civil war. A further 300,000 people disappeared, while 1 million Salvadorans left their country. El Salvador was a small country with only about 5.5 million people. The archbishop continued to speak out against the atrocities. On the night of March 24, 1980, Archbishop Romero celebrated his final Mass, a funeral Mass, at the hospital. He spoke to the deceased's relatives and friends:

> We know that every effort to better society,
> especially when injustice and sin are so ingrained,
> is an effort that God blesses,
>> that God wants,
>> that God demands of us.[18]

As he ended his homily, the archbishop was assassinated. The people were stunned. The following Sunday, March 30, 1980, more than fifty thousand people gathered in the square in front of the cathedral for his funeral Mass. While the people were singing and praying, someone tossed a number of small bombs into the crowd and utter panic broke out. Soldiers started shooting aimlessly. Some forty people were killed and hundreds were badly wounded. Archbishop John R. Quinn of the Archdiocese of San Francisco attended the funeral on behalf of the Catholic bishops of the United States. Archbishop Quinn described the event in this way:

> The Mass was on the front steps of the cathedral and was attended by many thousands of people. During the homily, given by the cardinal archbishop of Mexico City, a small bomb exploded, and after

a shot toward the back of the crowd, the shooting began in earnest. The frightened people broke ranks and poured frantically and uncontrollably through the open main doors into the cathedral. This second act of violence, at the homily, made the message plain that the church must stop speaking about justice and human rights.

Archbishop Romero saw the threat of death as a communion with the suffering Christ and predicted, "If they kill me, I will rise again in the Salvadoran people."[19]

Archbishop Romero's Spiritual Witness for Today

Archbishop Romero was a true pastoral leader. Originally, he shied away from involving himself in the political affairs of his nation. But, when he saw the atrocities perpetrated against his own people, he spoke out against them. He became the voice of the poor and the oppressed. Like Jesus in the gospels, he reached out to the marginalized of society. It took great courage and strength to stand against those who wielded power in society and to call them to account. As Archbishop Quinn said, Archbishop Romero saw the possibility of his own death, but this did not stop him from preaching the message of the gospel. The words that Jesus addressed to James and John in the Gospel of Mark speak just as clearly to the life of Archbishop Romero:

> "Can you drink the cup that I drink or be baptized with the baptism with which I am baptized?" They said to him, "We can." Jesus said to them, "The cup that I drink, you will drink, and with the baptism with which I am baptized, you will be baptized." (10:38-39)

Archbishop Romero remained true to the gospel of Jesus. As Jesus was put to death for the message he proclaimed, so Archbishop Romero followed in the Lord's footsteps and was assassinated for the same message. The grace of God's Spirit enabled him to remain faithful to his role as leader of his people and to embrace the cross of martyrdom.

Every Christian can derive inspiration from the life and martyrdom of Archbishop Romero. Like the archbishop, every Christian must work to name evil wherever it may be found. In his role as leader of his people, he spoke out like the prophets of the Old Testament: he challenged and condemned the atrocities perpetrated within his country. His courage and strength came from the power of God's Spirit. Archbishop Romero's commitment, strength, and humility inspire us in our own context to do what is within our power to challenge the injustices we see around us:

It is indeed a very great demand, but it is the demand of Jesus himself, re-spoken in the concrete historical context in which we live. As a Christian I am invited—yes, required—to work with all my energy for the salvation of the world. Oscar Romero makes it clear that such a work cannot be spiritualised: "All practices that disagree with the gospel must be removed if we are to save people. We must save not the soul at the hour of death but the person living in history."[20]

Embracing the Poor—Luke's Spirituality

The exploration of the spirituality of the Gospel of Luke revealed many important spiritual themes: the Christian life as a journey toward God, expressed in confident trust in God who offers salvation to all peoples through his Son's death and resurrection. Of singular significance for Luke's spirituality is his spiritual concern for the poor and the outcasts of society as Jesus demonstrated in his ministry. The two Christians I have chosen to illustrate Luke's spirituality both incarnate in their own lives this concern for the poor and outcasts of society, namely, St. Francis of Assisi and St. Damien of Molokai.

Saint Francis continues to exert an extraordinary influence upon the spirituality of the Christian church from his day until our own. Among the many dimensions of his spirituality, two are highlighted: his embodiment of a love for God's created world and his identification with the poor in the spirit of Luke's Jesus. An example of a more recent figure is St. Damien de Veuster, canonized by Pope Benedict XVI in 2009, the apostle to the leper colony on the island of Molokai (Hawaii). Damien's life exemplified the spirituality of Luke's Jesus by embracing those marginalized by society.

St. Francis of Assisi[21] *(1181/82–1226)*

Francis was born in the town of Assisi (Italy). His father was a wealthy textile merchant. Francis had a great sense of humor, loved to sing, and dressed in the best of clothes noted for their bright colors. When he was twenty years old, Francis took part in the fight between the cities of Assisi and Perugia. He was captured and imprisoned for a year. This experience prompted a slow reevaluation of his whole life and values. Many stories describe this ongoing process of change. His friends noted this transformation and thought that he was in love. Francis replied that "I am going to take a wife of surpassing beauty." Later, he would refer to her as "Lady Poverty," a phrase that Dante famously used in his *Divine Comedy.* One well-known story from Francis's early life tells about him praying before a crucifix in the small church of St. Damian below the town of Assisi when he heard the voice, "Go, Francis, and repair my house that is in ruins." Francis interpreted this message literally and set out to pay for the restoration of this church from his father's wealth. Pope Benedict has recently drawn attention to the symbolism of Francis's call:

> This simple occurrence of the word of God heard in the Church of St. Damian contains a profound symbolism. At that moment St. Francis was called to repair the small church, but the ruinous state of the building was a symbol of the dramatic and disquieting situation of the Church herself.[22]

This call was to symbolize the whole of Francis's life. His father was angry with him for spending too much of his wealth on the poor and brought him before the bishop. There Francis renounced his inheritance and tore off his clothes in a symbolic gesture that he would not take anything from his father. Standing there in his nakedness, he symbolized the original state of humanity before God. Francis embraced the life of a hermit. In 1208 while attending Mass, he heard the gospel text that encouraged the disciples to lay aside everything for their journey and to travel simply: Jesus "said to them [the Twelve], 'Take nothing for the journey, neither walking stick, nor sack, nor food, nor money, and let no one take a second tunic. Whatever house you enter, stay there and leave from there'" (Luke 9:1-4).

This text gave Francis his future mission: the call to embrace a life of poverty and to dedicate his life to preaching the word of God. Francis's future life was set in motion. He adopted the clothes of the local peasants, a gray woolen tunic around which he tied a knotted rope. Soon afterwards a number of followers joined him. In 1209 Francis went to Rome, where he told Pope Innocent III of his plan to found a new form of Christian life. The pope promised that when their numbers had increased, they would receive official approval.

Adopting a life of poverty, Francis and his followers embraced the spirit of the Jesus of the gospels who moved from place to place preaching the gospel message. Francis used the Portinuncula (the Church of Santa Maria degli Angeli) as their headquarters. There Francis welcomed Clare, a young woman from a rich family in Assisi, to follow his way of life. Clare in her turn attracted a number of followers; a "Second Franciscan Order" had started, namely, the Poor Clares.

One event in the life of Francis stands out as highly significant for our world today. Francis lived at a time of hostility between Christianity and Islam. In 1219 Francis met with the Muslim sultan Malik al-Klmil, who welcomed him graciously. The two had a pleasant discussion. In the following year, Francis visited the Holy Land. This event would foreshadow the special relationship that the followers of Francis, the Franciscans, have always had for the Holy Land. Today Franciscans have responsibility for caring for the sacred Christian places in the Holy Land. Like Francis, his followers have a significant relationship with the people of Islam.

A further important event in the life of Francis occurred on the feast of the Exaltation of the Cross, September 24, 1224. Francis had been fasting for forty days when he experienced a vision of the crucified Savior, appearing as a seraph (a six-winged angel) on the cross. This vision left Francis with the stigmata (wounds on his hands, feet, and side seeped blood). This experience demonstrated Francis's close identification with Christ and left him as a living representation of the crucified Lord.

Francis's health declined rapidly after this event. He returned to Assisi, where he spent his last days in a small hut. He died on October 3, 1226, in the place where his life and call began. He was canonized by Pope Gregory IX on July 16, 1228. The following day, the pope laid the foundation stone for a new church, the Basilica of St. Francis of Assisi.

St. Francis's Spirituality for Today

Francis's life and spirituality embody that of Jesus: his life of voluntary poverty, his clothes, his itinerant lifestyle, his life centered on prayer, his acceptance of fasting, and finally his very bodily stigmata. All these bear witness to the spirituality of Jesus of Nazareth, especially as Luke's gospel depicts it. The embrace of poverty ("Lady Poverty") reminded Christians of the thirteenth century, as it still does today, of the radical nature of the gospel of Jesus. Jesus identified himself in his birth and in his life with the poor. Francis followed Jesus' example. He urged his followers to embrace the virtue of poverty, both interiorly and exteriorly: "Blessed are you who are poor, for the kingdom of God is yours" (Luke 6:20).

The birth of Jesus as narrated in the Gospel of Luke provided Francis a further opportunity to draw attention to Jesus' poverty: "While they were there, the time came for Mary to have her child, and she gave birth to her firstborn son. She wrapped him in swaddling clothes and laid him in a manger, because there was no room for them in the inn" (2:6-7).[23] While paintings of the birth of Jesus had long been part of Christian tradition, Francis was the first to create a crèche or nativity scene by using live animals to give the effect of reality. Believers were able to meditate and reflect on the birth of Jesus in all its simplicity and its poverty. The scene consisted of a feeding trough with straw on which the Christ Child lay between a live ox and a donkey. This began the Christian tradition of building similar crèches in parish churches and in the homes of the faithful. These crèches strengthened the realization among believers that the Son of God was born among us in abject poverty. The Christ Child identified with our own poverty.

Not only did Francis's life and spirituality embrace the spirit of Jesus' endorsement of the love command, "You shall love the Lord, your God, with all your heart, with all your being, with all your strength, and with all your mind, and your neighbor as yourself" (Luke 10:27), but Francis also drew out the implications by showing that a love for God must always be expressed through a love for all people as well as a love for God's creation itself. This spirituality is expressed so beautifully in the well-known *Canticle of Creatures.* This is the first written piece of Italian literature and has been translated into almost every language. Francis expresses his spirituality so well by referring to God's creations as "Brother Fire" and "Sister Water" and to animals as "brothers and sisters of humanity." Today our world embraces more and more a need for the care and preservation of God's creation and the environment. All these efforts are in line with Francis's love for the world that God has created. In the spirit of St. Francis, Pope Benedict XVI in our day continues to call for a love and respect for God's creation:

> As I recalled in my recent Encyclical *Caritas in Veritate*, development is sustainable only when it respects Creation and does not damage the environment (cf. nn. 48-52), and in the Message for the World Day of Peace this year, I also underscored that even building stable peace is linked to respect for Creation. Francis reminds us that the wisdom and benevolence of the Creator is expressed through Creation. He understood nature as a language in which God speaks to us, in which reality becomes clear, and we can speak *of* God and *with* God.[24]

Finally in today's world where interaction and controversy occur between the major monotheistic religions, Francis's spirituality is worth noting. He approached the world of Islam, not with antagonism and hatred, but in a spirit of respect and love. His engagement with the Muslim sultan shows how barriers between peoples of different faiths can be broken down through honesty and respect for the other as a fellow creature of God. Our world can certainly take note of this spirituality of love and respect as a way of living with each another in peace and harmony.

Pope Benedict XVI sums up one significant aspect of the life and witness of St. Francis for our contemporary world:

> The witness of Francis, who loved poverty as a means to follow Christ with dedication and total freedom, continues to be for us too an invitation to cultivate interior poverty in order to grow in our trust of God, also by adopting a sober lifestyle and a detachment from material goods.[25]

Francis is as relevant today as he was for his thirteenth-century world, if not more so. His life and spirituality continue to challenge us through the spirit of the gospel to live in the spirit of the gospel message. By means of clearly articulated points, Francis's message transcends time and enables us to discover the value of an interior life of poverty that expresses itself in an attitude of indifference toward material goods.

St. Damien of Molokai (1840–1889)

Joseph de Veuster was born in Flanders, Belgium, on January 3, 1840. On joining the Congregation of the Sacred Hearts of Jesus and Mary, he received the religious name Damien. In 1864, at the age of twenty-three, Damien's congregation sent him as a missionary to the Kingdom of Hawaii. He was ordained a priest in Honolulu two months after his arrival and served on the island of Oahu for eight years.

In 1873, Damien volunteered for the leper colony on the island of Molokai. Hawaiians were susceptible to diseases brought to the island by foreigners. Leprosy was such a disease. To prevent leprosy spreading, King Kamehameha IV had confined the lepers to a colony on Molokai Island, where they were provided with food and clothing but little medical care. Damien remained there until his death sixteen years later. On the island, he cared for the spiritual as well as physical and medical needs of the eight hundred lepers living there.

Five years before his death, Damien contracted leprosy. He wrote that he did not wish to be cured if that would mean having to abandon his pastoral care for the lepers. Despite suffering from the disease, Damien continued to work until his death on April 15, 1889. His physical suffering was intensified through mental suffering when malicious rumors, accusing him of leading an immoral life, destroyed his good name.

He suffered further in his final years from rejection by his superiors. One can only imagine how abandoned and desolate Damien must have felt at his death. Investigations were made into all these allegations and Damien was thoroughly cleared some years after his death. The famous author Robert Louis Stevenson replied in a masterful way to the malicious accusations made by a Protestant minister, C. M. Hyde, against Fr. Damien.[26]

St. Damien's Spirituality for Today

The above brief exploration of St. Damien's life reveals someone open to God's guidance, leading him to serve the outcasts of society. The Gospel of Luke and the Acts of the Apostles present a spirituality whereby God's Spirit guides the spread of Jesus' message. In the same vein, looking back over the life of Fr. Damien, one can see that God's Spirit had guided this modern apostle to dedicate his life to God's service as a missionary. Like the apostles of old, he left his homeland of Flanders, Belgium, to go halfway across the world to the Kingdom of Hawaii. God's Spirit led him further to dedicate his life to the outcasts of society, to the lepers of Molokai.

Damien's spiritual concern for the poor and outcasts incarnated remarkably the spirituality of Luke's Jesus, who reached out to all those who were suffering, especially lepers, who came to him for healing. Just as the lepers of Jesus' time were forced to live outside the city and avoid contact with all people, so too the lepers of Hawaii had been banished to Molokai Island, where no one could see them or even be concerned about them.

Father Damien's spirituality was characterized by a life of total service and dedication. For sixteen years he gave himself to the spiritual and physical care of the lepers at Molokai. In this way, Damien imitated the life of service of Jesus, who gave himself totally to the service of humanity. Like Jesus, Damien's life of total dedication led ultimately to death. Jesus died after being falsely accused by the Jewish authorities and condemned by the Roman authorities. In like manner, Fr. Damien died with the knowledge that his whole life had been maliciously undermined by detractors and even believed by his own superiors!

As the Father vindicated his Son's death on behalf of humanity by raising Jesus from the dead, so would the life of Fr. Damien finally be justified. After a long process, Fr. Damien was canonized by Pope Benedict XVI on Sunday, October 11, 2009. At his canonization, Pope Benedict acknowledged the gift of St. Damien and held his life and spirituality up for imitation:

He [St. Damien] invites us to open our eyes to the forms of leprosy that disfigure the humanity of our brethren and still today
call for the charity of our presence as servants, beyond that of our
generosity.[27]

Today there is a cure for leprosy (Hansen's disease, as it is known
today). The life and spirituality of St. Damien remains as relevant as ever
for our world. As Pope Benedict XVI says so clearly, his life and spirituality are a challenge to all of us to embrace those in our society who
are marginalized, as were the lepers at the time of Jesus and St. Damien.
Our society may have cured the disease of leprosy that forced people to
be ostracized, but nevertheless the same stigma and rejection continues
today under other forms: people living with HIV/AIDS; legal and illegal
foreigners (whom our society labels as "Aliens"); people of another race,
religion, gender, or sexual orientation. Today, St. Damien is their patron
saint as he is for the state of Hawaii. Saint Damien's life and spirituality
serve as a very real and urgent reminder to us today, in the spirit of the
gospel, to accept, embrace, and care for all those ostracized by society
as our own brothers and sisters. Saint Damien has been memorialized
in bronze in the U.S. Capitol Statuary Hall, one of the two statues from
the state of Hawaii.

Grace, Contemplation, Love—John's Spirituality

The spirituality of the Gospel of John reflects a period of long contemplation on the mystery of the Word. This contemplation is rooted
in a personal relationship with God, a relationship lived together with
others who are also "children of God." The allegory of the vine and the
branches reflects well this relationship with the person of Jesus and our
interconnectedness with others. Love provides the foundation for the
relationship between Father, Son, and Holy Spirit and extends outward to
embrace believers. John's spirituality has inspired Christians throughout
the centuries. Through God's grace, many have emulated this intimate
spiritual relationship as illustrated in the life of the Beloved Disciple.
The two Christians selected here, St. Augustine of Hippo and St. Teresa
Benedicta of the Cross (Edith Stein), both illustrate God's grace drawing
them into this intimate relationship of love, giving their lives direction
and meaning. Like the gospel writer, their lives were spent contemplating and reflecting on the mystery of Jesus Christ and God's workings
in our world.

St. Augustine of Hippo (354–430)

Born in Thagaste (near Carthage in North Africa), Augustine's spiritual, theological, and philosophical writings are a watershed for Christianity and Western civilization. He brought the thought and culture of Greece and Rome into harmony with the Scriptures. Augustine was a prolific writer, preacher, and correspondent who left behind some 113 books, 200 letters, and over 800 sermons. Because of his insights into the wonders of God's grace working in the lives of humanity, Augustine has been recognized as one of the four great Doctors of the Catholic Church, under the title "Doctor of Grace."

God's Guiding Grace

Our exploration of Augustine's spirituality focuses chiefly on his *Confessions*. This work captures God's grace guiding him unexpectedly and unconsciously in his search for wisdom and truth. According to the custom of those days, Augustine was not baptized at birth. Nevertheless, his mother Monica immersed him as a child in her faith. Augustine writes, "Through your mercy, Lord, my tender little heart had drunk in that name [of Christ], the name of my Savior and your Son, with my mother's milk, and in my deepest heart I still held on to it" (*Conf.* 3.4.8).[28]

Despite Monica's deep faith, Augustine did not embrace the Christian faith. Instead, he sought to discover wisdom and truth for himself. His parents realized his intellectual gifts and sacrificed much to provide him with a first-rate education. Central to the education of that age was rhetoric, the art of persuasion. His parents sent Augustine to Carthage, where his studies in rhetoric flourished. His search for wisdom led him, at the age of nineteen, to embrace the Manichean religion, to which he belonged for almost ten years.

In Carthage, Augustine entered into a thirteen-year loving relationship, during which a child, Adeodatus ("gift of God"), was born. After completing his studies, Augustine taught rhetoric in Carthage. He later moved to Rome and then to Milan (the place of the Roman emperor), where he assumed the role of public orator.

Looking back over his life in his *Confessions*, Augustine sees God's grace leading him in unexpected and unconscious ways. In Milan, he heard of Bishop Ambrose's gift of rhetoric and went to listen to his preaching. Through Ambrose's sermons, Augustine became attracted to Christianity. At the same time, he discovered some books by the Platonists[29] that gave him new insights into God's spiritual nature. God's grace also led him to discover the letters of Paul. In discussions with friends, he also learned about the conversions of many people, such as Antony of Egypt (*Conf.* 8.6.14) and a certain Victorinus, who, like Augustine, was a well-respected rhetorician in Rome. Finally, God's grace led Augustine to a spiritual conversion in a Garden in Milan:

> Suddenly I heard a voice from a house nearby—perhaps a voice of some boy or girl, I do not know—singing over and over again, "Pick it up and read, pick it up and read." . . . Stung into action, I returned to the place where Alypius was sitting, for on leaving it I had put down there the book of the apostle's letters. I snatched it up, opened it and read in silence the passage on which my eyes first lighted: *Not in dissipation and drunkenness, nor in debauchery and lewdness, nor in arguing and jealousy; but put on the Lord Jesus Christ, and make no provision for the flesh or the gratification of your desires* [Rom 13:13-14]. I had no wish to read further, nor was there need. No sooner had I reached the end of the verse than the light of certainty flooded my heart and all dark shades of doubt fled away. (*Conf.* 8.12.29)[30]

Augustine was baptized by St. Ambrose in the Cathedral of Milan on Easter Sunday, April 24, 387, together with his friend Alypius and his son Adeodatus. God's grace continued to lead Augustine. Back home in Thagaste, Augustine founded a monastic community. Then in 391, while visiting the city of Hippo, Augustine was suddenly ordained a priest. While attending Mass, the bishop of Hippo expressed his need for an assistant priest who knew Latin well (as he, the bishop, was Greek). The people in the church immediately turned to Augustine and he was promptly ordained! Four years later in 395 Augustine was consecrated bishop of Hippo, a role he exercised until his death in 430. For those thirty-five years as bishop, Augustine continued to respond to God's grace as leader of God's people, and voice for the church in Africa. Through his writings, letters, and sermons, Augustine used the culture of Greece and Rome to explain and defend the Catholic faith against different groups that were undermining it.

God's Presence Within

In reflecting on his search for God, Augustine came to discover God's presence within him. He had been searching for God outside himself while God was always within him. One of his most beautiful prayers expresses this so vividly:

Late have I loved you, Beauty so ancient and so new,
late have I loved you!
Lo, you were within,
but I outside, seeking there for you,
and upon the shapely things you have made I rushed headlong,
I, misshapen.
You were with me, but I was not with you.
They held me back far from you,
those things which would have no being
were they not in you.
You called, shouted, broke through my deafness;
you flared, blazed, banished my blindness;
you lavished your fragrance, I gasped, and now I pant for you;
I tasted you, and I hunger and thirst;
you touched me, and I burned for your peace. (*Conf.* 10.27.38)[31]

Spirituality Imbued by the Word of God

Augustine's spirituality is above all a biblical spirituality. His *Confessions* are interwoven to such a degree with biblical quotations and images that he actually expresses his thoughts by means of the Scriptures. For Augustine, the Scriptures are God's love letter, as he intimates, "I love you, Lord, with no doubtful mind but with absolute certainty. You pierced my heart with your word, and I fell in love with you" (*Conf.* 10.6.8).[32]

Foundational for Augustine's spirituality are the letters of Paul, the Psalms, and especially the Gospel of John, the only gospel on which he wrote an entire commentary. The Gospel of John begins, "In the beginning was the Word, and the Word was with God" (1:1). For Augustine this title, the Word, was the fullest expression of Jesus as divine and human.

During his ministry as bishop of Hippo, the reading of the word of God at Mass provided Augustine with a source for reflecting upon and explaining God's word for his people. His hundreds of homilies that have been preserved testify to the depth of his insights and the importance and value that he gave to breaking the word of God for his people. The word of God is made present in the celebration of the sacraments.

Spirituality Centered on Love

Just as the Beloved Disciple in the Gospel of John witnessed to love as the center of a true disciple's relationship with Christ, so Augustine discovered in his own life that his relationship with Christ was founded upon love. In reading Augustine's *Confessions*, one realizes how intimately Augustine loves God. *The Confessions* give the impression that the reader is listening into a prayer to God in which Augustine lays bare his very essence.

In his reflections on the Gospel of John, Augustine notes that since the very life of God is love, all human relationships are founded on the life of God's love, the life of the relationships among the persons of the Trinity. Love for one's brothers and sisters is a share in God's intimate life, which is love.

The concept of friendship further illustrates our participation in the life of God's love. In the Gospel of John, Jesus refers to his disciples in this way: "You are my friends if you do what I command you. . . . I have called you friends because I have told you everything I have heard from my Father" (John 15:14-15). Jesus offers the grace of friendship to his followers and they in turn extend this friendship to others. Augustine reveals the depths of his friendship when he describes his overwhelming grief at the death of a very close friend when he was about twenty-one.[33]

Spirituality of Community

Augustine is never alone. He is always closely associated with his friends, his mother, and later his monastic community. Augustine's life shows that the Christian journey is not undertaken alone, but in communion with others. For Augustine, both the individual and the community dimensions of life are essential. The individual searches for God's presence, at the same time journeying with and being supported by others in the discovery of God's presence. Central to the life of the church is the life of community. Love requires a community. Together people search for wisdom and for the truth. This aim motivated Augustine to found a monastic community where every member could be supported in love by everyone else. In drawing up a Rule for his community, love was the bond that kept the community together: "First and foremost, my very dear Brothers, you are to love God, and then your neighbor, because these are the chief commandments given to us."[34]

St. Augustine's Spirituality for Today

While many sources from the classical and biblical worlds contributed to the development of Augustine's spirituality, the Gospel of John influenced his spirituality greatly. In John's gospel he saw reflected many of the essential ideas and beliefs that formed the heart of his spiritual vision. The concept of God as a God of love; the communication of this love to the individual; the presence of God within the soul of the individual; the indwelling of God as Father, Son, and Spirit; the understanding of Christ as the Word of God; and the importance of the life of the community—all these are vital to Augustine's spirituality and all are reflected so well within the Gospel of John.

Many aspects of Augustine's spirituality remain as relevant today as they were in his own day. For Augustine, life is a journey toward God, a journey in search of God. Augustine's spirituality is a thinking spirituality searching for meaning and wisdom in his life. His spirituality speaks well to the twenty-first century where people are searching individually to find meaning for their lives. The philosopher Charles Taylor describes the defining element of today's world as:

> The culture of "authenticity" . . . that each of us has his or her own way of realizing one's own humanity, and that it is important to find and live out one's own, as against surrendering to conformity.[35]

As Augustine's life embraced a spiritual journey seeking wisdom and truth, so young people's lives today are characterized by a similar spiritual journey. On this journey, Augustine offers today's generation a number of important guides. Most important of all is the awareness that the individual search for wisdom lies under the guiding hand of God's grace. This grace gives support and reassurance, especially when times are tough. However, this individualism needs to be tempered with a community dimension. The community offers support and guidance in the individual's search for God. As Augustine's community showed, their unity of mind and heart created an atmosphere that supported their search for God. Augustine's spiritual journey was always supported by others: his friends, his mother, his monastic community. They were his sustaining force. Their bonds of friendship enabled them to share themselves fully with each other. In our society today, there is need to develop again those close bonds of intimate friendship that will support us on our spiritual journey in search of God.

Edith Stein (St. Teresa Benedicta of the Cross [1891–1942])

Edith Stein was born to Jewish parents on the Day of Atonement, October 12, 1891, in Breslau (Germany). Her father died when she was two, leaving her mother to care for eleven children. Although Edith's mother was devout, Edith gave up her Jewish faith and belief in God as an adolescent.

On leaving high school, she enrolled at the University of Breslau and then in 1913 transferred to Göttingen University to study under Edmund Husserl, philosopher of phenomenology. Edith became Husserl's teaching assistant and obtained her doctorate in philosophy (summa cum laude) in 1917 for her thesis, "The Problem of Empathy." Despite her outstanding mind and scholarship, Edith's desire to get a position at a university was denied her on the basis that she was a woman and Jewish!

God's Grace, Her Guiding Force

In her studies as a philosopher, Edith Stein was searching for the truth. Her search, like that of St. Augustine, ultimately brought her to the Catholic Church. Looking back over her life, she saw the guiding light of God's grace leading her toward the Catholic Church. One of her first attractions to the Catholic Church occurred when she visited the Frankfurt Cathedral. While there, she noticed a woman with a shopping basket who had come into the cathedral to say a few prayers:

> This was something entirely new to me. To the synagogues or to the Protestant churches which I had visited, one went only for services. But, here was someone interrupting her everyday shopping errands to come into this church, although no other person was in it, as though she were here for an intimate conversation. I could never forget that.[36]

God's grace working in her life manifested itself so beautifully in 1921. While visiting some friends, she came across St. Teresa of Avila's autobiography. She spent the whole night reading. This experience changed her life. Through St. Teresa of Avila she had discovered truth. On January 1, 1922, Edith was baptized. Reflecting on this momentous event in her life, Edith made a connection to her Jewish roots and faith. Her baptism brought her into a relationship with Christ spiritually and ethnically.

Edith wanted to follow in the footsteps of St. Teresa of Avila and join a Carmelite Convent, but her spiritual director advised against it. Instead, she accepted a position at a Dominican teacher's training college in Speyer and also devoted herself to writing, translating (she translated the diaries and letters of Cardinal Newman into German), teaching, scholarship, and speaking, especially on issues related to women.

In 1933 when the Nazi persecution of the Jews began, her spiritual director supported her desire to join the Carmelites. On October 14,

1933, she entered the Discalced Carmelite Nuns' cloistered community in Cologne, taking the religious name of Sister Teresa Benedicta of the Cross. On Easter Sunday, April 21, 1935, she made her first profession of vows—her final profession was in 1938. In the Carmelite convent, she was given permission to continue her writing and scholarship. There she completed a work that she had begun years before on the concepts of Thomas Aquinas, *Potency and Act*. This work was to be her masterpiece, *Finite and Eternal Being*. However, because of anti-Semitism and the turmoil in Germany, she was not able to publish it.

Because her presence in the convent at Cologne put her community in danger, Sister Benedicta requested a transfer to a monastery outside Germany. On New Year's Eve, 1938, she crossed secretly into the Netherlands and was accepted into the Carmelite community in Echt. There she worked on a study on St. John of the Cross on the occasion of the four hundredth anniversary of his birth (1542–1942), titled *The Science of the Cross*. This would be her final book and remained uncompleted.

In May 1940, the Germans invaded the Netherlands. After the Nazis began deporting Jews to the death camps and Jewish children were being expelled from Catholic schools, the Dutch Catholic bishops responded with outrage. The bishops issued a letter that was read publicly in all the churches on July 20, 1942, in which they protested vehemently the Nazi treatment of Jews. In retaliation, the Nazis arrested all Catholics of Jewish descent. On August 2, Sister Teresa Benedicta was taken from the Carmelite convent in Echt by the Nazis, together with her sister Rosa who had also converted to Catholicism. Sister Benedicta and her sister were among 970 people of Jewish descent who were transported by cattle train to the death camp at Auschwitz. The trip was gruesome with many people dying on the way. On arriving at Auschwitz on August 9, 1942, Sister Benedicta and all who were with her died in the gas chambers.

Pope John Paul II beatified her in Cologne on May 1, 1987, and canonized her on October 11, 1998, in St. Peter's Square. In the following year, she was declared copatroness of Europe together with St. Bridget of Sweden and St. Catherine of Siena. She was the first Christian-Jewish martyr to be canonized since the time of the apostles.

Spirituality Embracing the World

As a philosopher, Edith Stein sought to describe the human person in relation to the world, not in opposition to or in conflict with it. The same was true of her spirituality. A person lives out the life of the spirit in the world and the significance of the world can only be grasped through an understanding of the human person. For her, God's action of salvation takes place within the world (see John 3:16-17). Her vision of engagement in the world runs totally counter to the spirituality of her time where the predominant viewpoint, especially for the contemplative life, was to guard oneself against the world, to draw oneself more and more out of and away from the world. Instead, she proposed a spirituality where God and humans encounter each other here in this world, not in some dimension withdrawn from the world. The spiritual is to be experienced and found in the ordinary world of ordinary people. As in the Gospel of John, Jesus encounters people in the course of their everyday occupations, the Samaritan woman at the well, the disciples in their fishing, the Beloved Disciple in the context of a meal.

As Edith Stein wrote to her friend Sister Callista on February 12, 1928:

> Immediately before, and for a good while after my conversion, I was of the opinion that to lead a religious life meant one had to give up all that was secular and to live totally immersed in thoughts of the Divine. But gradually I realized that something else is asked of us in this world and that, even in the contemplative life, one may not sever the connection with the world. I believe that the deeper one is drawn into God, the more one must "go out of oneself"; that is, one must go to the world in order to carry the divine life into it.[37]

Edith's spirituality encouraged Christians to use their gifts in the service of making God known. Her vision was that the human person was "only an instrument through whom God works in the world."[38]

A Woman's Spirituality

Edith Stein was excluded from professorships at universities solely because she was a woman. Those experiences did not leave her bitter or resentful. Instead, she used every opportunity to foster the role of women in society. She was invited to speak at numerous organizations of women where she addressed those issues that specifically pertained to women. In 1928, she addressed the Bavarian Catholic Women Teachers Association on the topic, "Woman's intrinsic value in national Life." Contrary to some groups of the time (such as the suffragettes), Edith Stein argued for "a feminine singularity." By this she understood the unique characteristics and intrinsic value that define a woman in distinction to a man. For her, man was more objective, while woman embraced a more personal attitude where "she has particular interest for the living, concrete person, and, indeed, as much for her own personal life and personal affairs as for those of other persons."[39]

For Edith Stein, Mary, the Mother of Jesus, held a special place as an example for women to imitate:

> But just as grace cannot achieve its work in souls unless they open themselves to it in free decision, so also Mary cannot function fully as a mother if men do not entrust themselves to her. Those women who wish to fulfill their feminine vocations in one of several ways will most surely succeed in their goals . . . if they also entrust themselves to her guidance and place themselves completely under her care. She herself can form in her own image those who belong to her.[40]

Spirituality of the Cross

A focal point of John's spirituality was the grace of Jesus drawing people into relationship with him. This is also the essence of the life of Edith Stein. Like Augustine, she too was searching for the truth and slowly God's grace drew her to his Son. By becoming a Catholic, Edith embraced the cross of Jesus and followed Jesus to death. A poem she wrote in 1938, "To Stand at the Cross," shows her willingness to share in the cross of Christ. She sees the acceptance of the cross in life as a condition for participating in the eternal glory with God. For Jesus in the Gospel of John, the cross was the path to return to the Father and the glory he had with God from the beginning: "I glorified you on earth by accomplishing the work that you gave me to do. Now, glorify me, Father, with you, with the glory that I had with you before the world began" (John 17:4-5). For Edith Stein as well, the cross of Jesus was the path to return to the Father. In this poem, Edith Stein imagines that she stands with Mary at the foot of the cross as John's gospel narrates (19:25-27). Those who are to share in the glory of the future kingdom must first stand beneath Jesus' cross and like Jesus their sufferings and pains will "purchase heavenly glory" for those who are entrusted to their care. She offers an important insight that we share in Christ's death on behalf of others, especially those to whom we minister.[41]

St. Teresa Benedicta's Spirituality for Today

Like Augustine, Sister Teresa Benedicta is an inspiration for young people today who are searching for the truth. Her life witnesses to the power of grace working in the life of one who seeks the truth. Grace led her to the discovery of an intimate relationship with God through Christ. As the Gospel of John endeavored to draw out Jesus' relationship with women and showed their equality and vitality in his ministry, so the writings of Sister Teresa Benedicta on the "feminine singularity" are an inspiration to women today. Like the Beloved Disciple, her life was a constant contemplation of the significance of Christ for herself and for all humanity. Through her contemplation and philosophical inquiry pursued under God's grace, she saw that we "may never sever the connection with the world." The world is where God's salvation occurs and we have to work out our salvation in the world through the grace of Christ. Hers is a spirituality not of flight from the world but of engagement with the world. Such a spirituality reflects the energies of young people today for whom the world as the place of God's creation is where they discover God's presence and use their talents in the service of one another. She bore witness to the world in two ways: her philosophical inquiries shed light on the human person in relationship to the world. Secondly, her own death witnessed to her beliefs and her identification with Jesus on the cross. Her religious name is a powerful reminder of how she embraced the cross of suffering and death in union with Christ.

Conclusion

The lives of Augustine and Edith Stein demonstrate a number of fascinating similarities:

a search for Truth, God, and the meaning of life

the power of God's guiding grace

a journey in discovering God's presence in their lives

a mystical spirituality

pursuit of a life of philosophical inquiry that drew them to Christ, and through their philosophy they endeavored to explain their Christian faith

'the witness of certain saints' lives drew them to the Catholic Church

a strong connection with the Gospel of John: an intense love for a relationship with the risen Christ

While the spirituality of the Gospel of John strongly emphasizes the personal bonds between the Father and the Son, it also embraces a very strong community dimension where the lives of believers are invited to share in the life of the Father, Son, and Spirit. Saint Augustine saw the need to establish a community where the love of God could be embraced more fully and shared together with others in the same quest for God's love and presence in their lives. Saint Teresa Benedicta was also drawn to the life of contemplation in community with others.

Together Augustine and Edith Stein witness to the long spiritual tradition of the importance of contemplation and the discovery of God's presence working within our lives and within our world. The gift of God's grace led them both unconsciously to embrace the Catholic faith. All efforts to touch the life of our world stem from the power of God's grace communicated to us through the death and resurrection of Christ.

CHAPTER SEVEN

Conclusion:
The Spiritual Journey Continues

By now the reader will appreciate the richness and diversity of the spiritual vision of the Scriptures and how that vision transformed the lives of Christians over the centuries. Our exploration of the spirituality of the gospels has drawn out their spiritual vision from its incarnation within the historical culture and worldview of the New Testament. Such is the very nature of the Sacred Scriptures, taken seriously as God's word, spoken through human words, at a particular time, and within a particular culture. God's word was intended to have meaning for all people at all times and within all cultures. Consequently, we have also shown how it was later incarnated within new historical cultures and worldviews and how it needs to be incarnated anew today.

We defined Christian spirituality as, "The search to integrate life through the transforming experience of encountering God in Christ. This experience animates and gives life meaning and direction."[1] Each gospel writer illustrated how the experience of encountering God in Christ transforms the lives of believers and challenges them to respond with a new way of life.

Our world with its diversity of worldviews differs greatly from that of the world of the Old and New Testaments. However, in the modern Western world of the twenty-first century, there are some characteristics that define the essence of the modern identity. The culture that characterizes today's Western world has been defined as a "culture of authenticity" that Charles Taylor explains in this way:

> I mean the understanding of life that emerged with the Romantic
> expressivism of the late eighteenth century, that each of us has his

or her own way of realizing one's own humanity, and that it is important to find and live out one's own, as against surrendering to conformity.[2]

Significant in Taylor's portrait of the modern world's culture of authenticity is his view that religion or belief cannot be imposed from outside on the individual or on the community. Each person undertakes an individual spiritual journey and one cannot simply be made to conform to the dictates of society or of religion. In our culture, "the religious life or practice that I become part of not only must be my choice, but must speak to me; it must make sense in terms of my spiritual development as I understand this."[3]

Because it gives meaning and direction to "my spiritual development," the freedom to choose is to be embraced as the reality of the present. The freedom to choose is at the very heart of the Christian tradition. This is evident from the very beginning. In the Gospel of John, Jesus offers a long discourse on the "Bread of Life" (chap. 6), where he explains to his hearers the significance of his identification as "I am the bread of life" (John 6:48). Many of Jesus' hearers found these words hard to accept and left him. Jesus then turns to the Twelve and asks them, "Do you also want to leave?" to which Simon Peter replied, "Master, to whom shall we go? You have the words of eternal life. We have come to believe and are convinced that you are the Holy One of God" (John 6:67-69). Peter and the others freely choose to stay with Jesus because they see that what he says and who he is makes total sense in their spiritual development. Nothing else can equal what Jesus is for their spiritual life. This challenges the reader and invites the reader to make a similar response.

As noted in the opening chapter,[4] the spirituality of the gospels must be encountered in ways that speak to the individual's inner self, giving it meaning and direction. The individual spiritual journey must be respected and encouraged. At the same time, one never journeys alone. The journey always occurs in connection with others. In the context of the spiritual faith journey, it occurs especially within a community of faith that supports, inspires, and guides the Christian on the spiritual journey. Quoting again Archbishop Wilson:

> In an expressivist age, believers must recognize the individual quest of every person and lead each one to discover the Gospel as God's clearest word about their lives and the community of Jesus' disciples as the place where his life is made most manifest in the world today.[5]

At the conclusion to the exploration of each gospel's spiritual vision, we pointed to aspects of the spiritual vision that speak to today's world. We endeavored to show how that gospel vision can be embraced today with its focus more on the *interior spiritual life*. However, that focus does not exclude what we have noted consistently throughout each chapter, that our world is also one where there is a deep consciousness of our common humanity. This common humanity inspires believers to search for ways, in the spirit of Jesus, to show concern for those who are especially in need, the outcasts of society and to champion those who are defenseless.

As Antony embraced aspects of the spirituality of Matthew's gospel and adopted a spiritual, ascetical life, he gave birth in the Western church to the *tradition of monasticism*. Monasticism has continued to exercise an important role in the life of the Catholic Church, transforming the lives of individuals and the church as a whole. Dorothy Day, also inspired by aspects of the spirituality of Matthew's gospel, has shown us a tradition that has been consciously embraced more and more over the past century: *the heart of spirituality requires openness to the needs of the poor.* She shows us another important spiritual tradition within the community of faith, namely, that all social action starts with, and is inspired by, the vision and teachings of the Scriptures.

The Gospel of Mark, with its focus on the *spirituality of martyrs*, has handed on to the community of faith the significance and importance of martyrdom. The Christian church has always flourished through the blood of martyrs. Perpetua, Felicity, and Archbishop Romero are examples that are highly significant and characteristic of a spiritual tradition that imitated Jesus' life in the fullest possible way by dying for what they believed. From the first centuries, Christians acknowledged the significance of the lives and deaths of martyrs. This spiritual tradition continues today. The past century has witnessed numerous Christians suffering and dying for their beliefs.

Saint Francis of Assisi was inspired by the Gospel of Luke to embrace the spirit of Jesus who led a life of poverty and moved from place to place preaching the gospel message. Through his group of faithful followers, attracted by his lifestyle, Francis handed on the *spiritual tradition of voluntary poverty* that has always energized the lives of many Christians, both individually, and as members of communities who have dedicated themselves to the service of others through lives of spiritual poverty. Francis's message would clearly challenge today's consumer-dominated society to adopt a different attitude toward material goods.

Further, Francis's love for the world that God created is a wonderful inspiration for our present world in its noble efforts to preserve God's creation and the environment.

The life of St. Damien of Molokai captured that spiritual tradition of Luke's Jesus who embraced the outcasts of society. Saint Damien shows us today how this *spiritual outreach to the marginalized* of society lies at the heart of Jesus' spirituality and is extremely significant in today's world where so many people are living with HIV/AIDS, or are foreigners or refugees living within another society or culture.

John's gospel is characterized by a spirituality of reflection on the significance of the life and message of Jesus. As such, John's gospel has given rise to a *spiritual tradition of contemplation* that has been ever significant and characteristic of Catholic spirituality. Saint Augustine's life is energized by, and testifies to, the handing on of this spiritual tradition. His life was guided by the awareness that an individual's life is under the guiding hand of *God's grace.* Augustine's search for meaning and wisdom was a lifelong journey, reflecting and contemplating on the word of God. At the same time, he was supported by the lives and friendship of others on his spiritual journey.

Edith Stein's (St. Teresa Benedicta of the Cross) search for wisdom and truth, like Augustine, is without doubt an important inspiration for young people today who are searching in a similar vein for guidance and wisdom in their lives. Her life is a testimony to a *spirituality of grace.* God's grace led her on her journey to embrace first of all the message of Christianity, then a life of contemplation with the Carmelites, and finally the cross.

These examples do not exhaust the spiritual vision of the Scriptures. Many other spiritual traditions could also be identified from the richness of the Christian spiritual legacy of the past two thousand years. The examples chosen are characteristic of some of the most significant spiritual traditions within the Catholic heritage. They were ordinary people, like you and me, with individual personalities, strengths, and weaknesses. The power of God's Spirit incarnated that scriptural vision in their lives. While this appropriation was important for the individuals themselves, at the same time their transformation gave an impetus to others to embrace the tradition and to hand it on to future generations. The lives of these witnesses show how certain spiritual traditions developed out of the spiritual vision of the Scriptures and continue to be as relevant today as they ever were. As in the past, so too today, the spiritual vision of the Scriptures continues to transform the lives of believers. As Vatican II said:

All the preaching of the Church, as indeed the entire Christian religion, should be nourished and ruled by sacred Scripture. In the sacred books the Father who is in heaven comes lovingly to meet his children, and talks with them. And such is the force and power of the Word of God that it can serve the Church as her support and vigor, and the children of the Church as strength for their faith, food for the soul, and a pure and lasting fount of spiritual life. Scripture verifies in the most perfect way the words: "The Word of God is living and active" (Heb. 4:12), and "is able to build you up and to give you the inheritance among all those who are sanctified" (Acts 20:32; cf. 1 Th. 2:13).[6]

Endnotes

Introduction—pages xi–xiii

1. For a brief survey of the history of spirituality, see Sandra Schneiders, "Theology and Spirituality: Strangers, Rivals, or Partners?" *Horizons* (Villanova) 13/2 (1986): 253–74.

2. See *Dei Verbum* (The Dogmatic Constitution on Divine Revelation) from the Second Vatican Council, as well as the document from the Pontifical Biblical Commission titled The Interpretation of the Bible in the Church (1993).

3. Joseph Ratzinger (Pope Benedict XVI) expresses this thought concisely in his book *Jesus of Nazareth: From the Baptism in the Jordan to the Transfiguration* ([New York: Doubleday, 2007], xv): "The first point is that the historical-critical method—specifically because of the intrinsic nature of theology and faith—is and remains an indispensable dimension of exegetical work. For it is of the very essence of biblical faith to be about real historical events. It does not tell stories symbolizing suprahistorical truths, but is based on history, history that took place here on this earth. The *factum historicum* (historical fact) is not an interchangeable symbolic cipher for biblical faith, but the foundation on which it stands: *Et incarnatus est*—when we say these words, we acknowledge God's entry into real history."

Chapter One—pages 1–10

1. *Random House Webster's College Dictionary* (New York: Random House, 1995), 1291.

2. Sandra Schneiders, "Theology and Spirituality: Strangers, Rivals, or Partners?" *Horizons* (Villanova) 13/2 (1986): 266.

3. Gustavo Gutierrez is a well-known liberation theologian. *We Drink from Our Own Wells: The Spiritual Journey of a People*, trans. Matthew J. O'Connell (Maryknoll, NY: Orbis Books, 1985), 52.

4. Ibid., 53.

5. *Dei Verbum* (The Dogmatic Constitution on Divine Revelation of the Second Vatican Council) drew attention to this: "But since sacred Scripture must be read and interpreted with its divine authorship in mind, no less attention must be devoted to the content and unity of the whole of Scripture, taking into account the Tradition of the entire Church and the analogy of faith, if we are to derive their true meaning from the sacred texts" (Austin Flannery, OP, ed., *Vatican Council II: Volume 1, The Conciliar and Post Conciliar Documents* [Northport, NY: Costello, 1996], par. 12, 758).

6. Paul Ricoeur, *Interpretation Theory: Discourse and the Surplus of Meaning* (Fort Worth, TX: Texas Christian University Press, 1976), 92, italics mine.

7. The phrase "expressivist age" is one that Charles Taylor (a Canadian Catholic philosopher and emeritus professor of philosophy at McGill University) used to capture one aspect of the identity of contemporary Western people. For Taylor, Westerners realize their identity through self-expression. (See Charles Taylor, "The Expressivist Turn," chap. 21, in *Sources of the Self: The Making of the Modern Identity"* [Cambridge, MA: Harvard University Press, 1989], 368–90.)

8. Archbishop Philip Wilson, "Shaping the Future of the Church," *Origins* (May 2007): 41.

Chapter Two—pages 13–29

1. I use the term "Matthew" (and likewise with the other gospels) to refer to the author of the Gospel of Matthew. In doing so, I do not wish to enter into the discussion of who the actual author of the gospel was.

2. The symbol "Q" is an abbreviation for the German word *Quelle*, which means "source." It refers to a hypothetical source that the gospels of Matthew and Luke used in the composition of their gospels. This hypothesis has been accepted by the majority of scholars over the past 150 years. This source is judged to be totally independent of Mark's gospel. For a good explanation of Q, I refer you to John S. Kloppenborg, *Q, The Earliest Gospel: An Introduction to the Original Stories and Sayings of Jesus* (Louisville, KY: Westminster John Knox Press, 2008).

3. In Scripture references, italics are mine.

4. See *"genesis,"* in *A Greek-English Lexicon of the New Testament and other Early Christian Literature*, 3rd ed., revised and edited by Frederick William Danker, based on Walter Bauer's *Griechisch-deutsches Wörterbuch den Schriften des Neuen Testaments und der frühchristlichen Literatur*, 6th ed., ed. Kurt Aland and Barbara Aland, with Viktor Reichmann; and on previous English editions by W. F. Arndt, F. W. Gingrich, and F. W. Danker (Chicago and London: The University of Chicago Press, 2000), 192–93.

5. *"Proskyneō,"* in ibid., 882.

6. Note that Matthew does not have the language of the later councils of the Church to refer to God as one being in three persons. The belief is evident here but it lacks the precision of later centuries.

7. For a detailed discussion on the concept of "perfection" in the New Testament and especially its usage in the Gospel of Matthew, see Patrick J. Hartin, *A Spirituality of Perfection: Faith in Action in the Letter of James* (Collegeville, MN: Liturgical Press, 1999).

8. Ibid., 33.

9. Daniel J. Harrington, SJ, *The Gospel of Matthew*, Sacra Pagina Series, vol. 1 (Collegeville, MN: Liturgical Press, 1991), 360.

Chapter Three—pages 30–43

1. As noted in chapter 2, note 6, Mark's usage of language in speaking about God, like Matthew, is not informed by the language of Chalcedon. Mark does not speak about an ontological relationship between Jesus and the Father. When Mark speaks about God he has in mind the Father as Matthew was intent on referring to God. Mark's Jesus refers to God in this way. For example, at the Garden of Gethsemane, Jesus says, "Abba, Father, all things are possible to you" (Mark 14:36).

2. The words "the Son of God" are placed in brackets in the NAB translation. The translators wanted to indicate that these words are missing in a number of ancient manuscripts. But evidence for their presence in other ancient manuscripts is "extremely strong" (see Bruce M. Metzger, *A Textual Commentary on the Greek New Testament*, corrected ed. [London/New York: United Bible Societies, 1975], 73).

3. For a more detailed examination of this section and the Gospel of Mark itself, see Robert Kugler and Patrick Hartin, "Chapter 49: The Gospel of Mark," in *An Introduction to the Bible* (Grand Rapids, MI/Cambridge, UK: Eerdmans, 2009), 370-72.

4. Ibid., 374–75.

5. Pope John Paul II, Apostolic Letter, *"Tertio Millennio Adveniente of his Holiness Pope John Paul II to the Bishops, Clergy and Lay Faithful on Preparation for the Jubilee of the Year 2000,"* paragraph 37. Issued from the Vatican, November 10, 1994 (http://www.vatican.va/holy_father/john_paul_ii/apost_letters/documents/hf_jp-ii_apl_10111994_tertio-millennio-adveniente_en.html).

Chapter Four—pages 44–58

1. Other examples of biblical books that were divided into two parts in a similar way are 1 and 2 Samuel, 1 and 2 Kings, and 1 and 2 Chronicles. These books were originally one work that was divided into two parts out

of necessity. For one of the best explanations of the production of ancient books, see Bruce M. Metzger, "The Making of Ancient Books," chapter 1 in *The Text of the New Testament: Its Transmission, Corruption and Restoration*, 2nd ed. (Oxford: Clarendon Press, 1968), 3–35.

2. Fulton J. Sheen, *Guide to Contentment* (Canfield, OH: Alba House, St Pauls, 1996), 174.

3. Stephen C. Barton, *The Spirituality of the Gospels* (Peabody, MA: Hendrickson Publishers, 1992), 104.

Chapter Five—pages 59–72

1. The first Church historian, Eusebius, notes that Clement of Alexandria (ca. AD 150–213) was the first person to coin the phrase "the spiritual gospel" in reference to the Gospel of John: "John, last of all, conscious that the outward facts had been set forth in the Gospels, was urged on by his disciples, and divinely moved by the Spirit, composed a spiritual Gospel. This is Clement's account" (J. E. L. Oulton, *Eusebius: The Ecclesiastical History*, vol. II, 6.14.7 [Cambridge, MA: Harvard University Press, 1956], 48–49).

2. In the Greek world, the Stoic philosophers spoke of the *Logos* that referred to the creative power that brought order into a chaotic world and was accessible to human reason. In the Hebrew world, a wisdom tradition had introduced a divine figure, *Sophia* (the Greek word for wisdom), who was with God in the creation of the world (see wisdom passages such as Sir 24; Wis 6:12–10:21; and Prov 8:1-36). Both these sources are reflected in the writings of the Jewish philosopher Philo (20 BC– AD 50), who lived in Alexandria, Egypt. He used the term *Logos* to refer to the image of God that served as a template for God's creation of the world. The *Logos* was also the instrument by which God effected the creation. For Philo, God created the *Logos* first and then the *Logos* in turn brought the rest of creation into being.

3. There are seven of these "I am sayings." The other six sayings are:

> *"I am the light of the world.* Whoever follows me will not walk in darkness, but will have the light of life" (8:12). The following of Jesus illuminates the pathway to salvation.
>
> *"I am the gate for the sheep"* (10:7). For salvation, everyone has to pass through Jesus, the gate.
>
> *"I am the good shepherd.* A good shepherd lays down his life for the sheep" (10:11). Jesus protects those who follow him to the extent of giving his life in death for them.
>
> *"I am the resurrection and the life*; whoever believes in me, even if he dies, will live" (11:25). For those who believe in him Jesus promises a life after death that will never end.

"*I am the way and the truth and the life.* No one comes to the Father except through me" (14:6). Jesus states unambiguously here what the gospel identifies as Jesus' whole aim: to reveal the Father. He alone can reveal the Father fully because he is the Son.

"*I am the true vine, and my Father is the vine grower*" (15:1). While Jesus is the vine, believers are the branches. It is vital for believers to remain united to the vine if they are to continue to live.

4. Barbara E. Bowe, *Biblical Foundations of Spirituality: Touching a Finger to the Flame* (Lanham, MD: Rowman & Littlefield Publishers, 2003), 148.

5. *Louō*, "(1) to use water to cleanse a body of physical impurity, wash . . . (2) to use water in a cultic manner for purification, wash oneself, bathe oneself" (*A Greek-English Lexicon of the New Testament and other Early Christian Literature*, 3rd ed. [BDAG], revised and ed. Frederick William Danker, based on Walter Bauer's *Griechisch-deutsches Wörterbuch zu den Schriften des Neuen Testaments und der früchristlichen Literatur*, 6th ed., ed. Kurt Aland and Barbara Aland, with Viktor Reichmann and on previous English editions by W. F. Arndt, F. W. Gingrich, and F. W. Danker [Chicago and London: The University of Chicago Press, 2000], 603).

6. *Paraklētos*, "In the few places where the word is found in pre-Christian and extra-Christian literature as well it has for the most part a more general sense: *one who appears in another's behalf, mediator, intercessor, helper.* . . . In our literature the active sense *helper, intercessor* is suitable in all occurrences of the word" (*A Greek-English Lexicon*, 766).

7. Raymond E. Brown, *The Gospel and Epistles of John: A Concise Commentary* (Collegeville, MN: Liturgical Press, 1988), 86–87.

8. R. Alan Culpepper, *Anatomy of the Fourth Gospel: A Study in Literary Design* (Philadelphia: Fortress Press, 1983), 124.

Part Two—page 73

1. See Pope Benedict's General Audience on Wednesday, January 27, 2010, on Saint Francis of Assisi (http://www.vatican.va/holy_father/benedict_xvi/audiences/2010/documents/hf_ben-xvi_aud_20100127_en.html).

Chapter Six—pages 75–104

1. Robert T. Meyer, trans., St. Athanasius: *The Life of Saint Antony*, Ancient Christian Writers Series (Westminster, MD: Newman Press, 1950), 17.

2. *Random House: Webster's College Dictionary* (New York: Random House, 1995), 79.

3. Meyer, *Life of Saint Antony*, 19.

4. Ibid., 97.

5. *Webster's College Dictionary*, 79.

6. See Dorothy Day, *The Long Loneliness: The Autobiography of Dorothy Day* (New York: Harper and Brothers, 1952), 45.

7. Ibid., 25.

8. Ibid., 107.

9. Ibid., 141.

10. Ibid., 166.

11. Ibid., 205.

12. Alexander Roberts and James Donaldson, eds., "The Martyrdom of Perpetua and Felicitas," Appendix V, in *The Ante-Nicene Fathers: Translations of the Writings of the Fathers down to A.D. 325*, Vol. III, trans. R. E. Wallis, 697–706 (New York: Charles Scribner's Sons, 1903).

13. Ibid., 699–700.

14. Ibid., 700.

15. Ibid., 705.

16. These words are from Archbishop Romero's sermon of December 18, 1977. See James R. Brockman, compiler and translator, *The Church Is All of You: Thoughts of Archbishop Oscar Romero* (Minneapolis: Winston Press, 1984), 17.

17. Ibid., 5.

18. Ibid., 110.

19. John R. Quinn, Archbishop, "The Relation of Moral Life and Moral Laws," *Origins* (May 30, 1996): 29.

20. Henri J. M. Nouwen, foreword to Brockman, *The Church Is All of You*, ix.

21. See Pope Benedict XVI, General Audiences on Wednesdays, January 13 and 27, 2010, where he refers to St. Francis of Assisi: (http://www.vatican .va/holy_father/benedict_xvi/audiences/2010/documents/hf_ben-xvi_ aud_20100113_en.html; http://www.vatican.va/holy_father/benedict_xvi/ audiences/2010/documents/hf_ben-xvi_aud_20100127_en.html).

22. See Pope Benedict XVI, General Audience on Wednesday, January 27, 2010.

23. Matthew, on the other hand, implies that Jesus was born in a house. Matthew tells the story of how the magi were led by a star to where the Christ Child was after his birth: "And behold, the star that they had seen at its rising preceded them, until it came and stopped over the place where the child was. They were overjoyed at seeing the star, and on entering the *house* they saw the child with Mary his mother" (Matt 2:9-11).

24. Pope Benedict XVI, General Audience on Wednesday, January 27, 2010.

25. Ibid.

26. Robert Louis Stevenson, *Father Damien: An Open Letter to the Reverend Doctor Hyde of Honolulu from Robert Louis Stevenson* (London: Chatto and Windus, 1914). C. M. Hyde had written a letter against Fr. Damien in Honolulu on August 2, 1889, some four months after Fr. Damien's death. The letter was published in the Sydney Presbyterian on October 26, 1889. Robert Louis Stevenson (author of the famous *Treasure Island*), who had visited the island after Fr. Damien's death, responded to this defamatory letter and supported Fr. Damien with an open letter of his own on February 25, 1890. It was subsequently reprinted in book form in 1914.

27. Pope Benedict XVI, homily on the occasion of the canonization of St. Damien together with four other new saints on Sunday October 11, 2009, at the Vatican Basilica (www.vatican.va/holy_father/benedict_xvi/homilies/2009/documents/hf_ben-xvi_hom_20091011_canizzazioni_en.html).

28. Maria Boulding, OSB, *Saint Augustine: The Confessions. I/1.* The Works of Saint Augustine: A Translation for the 21st Century (Hyde Park, NY: New City Press, 1997), 80.

29. Ibid., 169–70: "you provided me with some books by the Platonists, translated from the Greek into Latin. In them I read (not that the same words were used, but precisely the same doctrine was taught, buttressed by many and various arguments) that *in the beginning was the Word, and the Word was with God; he was God*" (*Conf.* 7.9.13).

30. Ibid., 206–7.

31. Ibid., 262.

32. Ibid., 241.

33. Ibid., 101 (*Conf.* 4,9.14).

34. Prologue to "The Rule of St. Augustine," in Mary T. Clark, trans., *Augustine of Hippo: Selected Writings* (Mahwah, NJ: Paulist Press, 1984), 485.

35. Charles Taylor, *Varieties of Religion Today: William James Revisited* (Cambridge, MA: Harvard University Press, 2002), 83.

36. Josephine Koeppel, OCD, trans., *Life in a Jewish Family: Her Unfinished Autobiographical Account*, The Collected Works of Edith Stein, vol. 1. Translation of *Aus dem Leben einer Jüdischen Familie, Das Leben Edith Stein: Kindheit und Jugend* (Washington, DC: ICS Publications, 1986), 401.

37. Josephine Koeppel, OCD, trans., *Self-Portrait in Letters: 1916–1942*, The Collected Works of Edith Stein, vol. 5. Translation of *Selbstbildnis in Briefen* (Washington, DC: ICS Publications, 1993), 54.

38. Ibid., 54–55.

39. Quoted in John Sullivan, OCD, *Edith Stein: Essential Writings*, Modern Spiritual Masters Series (Maryknoll, NY: Orbis Books, 2002), 98.

40. Freda Mary Oben, trans., *Essays on Woman.* The Collected Works of Edith Stein, vol. 2 (Washington, DC: ICS Publications, 1987), 234.

41. For the text of this poem, "To Stand at the Cross" (*Iuxta Crucem Tecum Stare*), see Sullivan, *Edith Stein: Essential Writings*, 127.

Chapter Seven—pages 105–9

1. See chapter 1, p. 6.

2. Charles Taylor, *Varieties of Religion Today: William James Revisited* (Cambridge, MA: Harvard, 2002), 83.

3. Ibid., 94.

4. See chapter 1, pp. 8–10.

5. Archbishop Philip Wilson, "Shaping the Future of the Church," *Origins* (May 2007): 41.

6. Austin Flannery, OP, ed., Dogmatic Constitution on Divine Revelation (*Dei Verbum*), *Vatican Council II: Volume 1, The Conciliar and Post Conciliar Documents* (Northport, NY: Costello, 1996), par. 21, 762.

Bibliography

Balthasar, Hans Urs von. "The Gospel as Norm and Test of All Spirituality in the Church." *Concilium* 9 (1965): 14–17.

Barton, Stephen C. *The Spirituality of the Gospels*. Peabody, MA: Hendrickson Publishers, 1992.

Boulding, Maria, OSB. *Saint Augustine: The Confessions*. I/1. The Works of Saint Augustine: A Translation for the 21st Century. Hyde Park, NY: New City Press, 1997.

Bowe, Barbara E. *Biblical Foundations of Spirituality: Touching a Finger to the Flame*. A Sheed & Ward Book. Lanham, MD: Rowman & Littlefield Publishers, 2003.

Brockman, James R., trans. *The Church Is All of You: Thoughts of Archbishop Oscar Romero*. Minneapolis: Winston Press, 1984.

Brown, Raymond E. *The Gospel and Epistles of John: A Concise Commentary*. Collegeville, MN: Liturgical Press, 1988.

Callahan, Annice, RSCJ. "The Relationship between Spirituality and Theology." *Horizons* 16, no. 2 (1989): 266–74.

Clark, Mary T., trans. "The Rule of St. Augustine." In *Augustine of Hippo: Selected Writings*. Mahwah, NJ: Paulist Press, 1984.

Conn, Joann Wolski, ed. *Women's Spirituality: Resources for Christian Development*. New York: Paulist, 1986.

Culpepper, R. Alan. *Anatomy of the Fourth Gospel: A Study in Literary Design*. Philadelphia: Fortress Press, 1983.

Cunningham, Lawrence S., and Keith J. Egan. *Christian Spirituality: Themes from the Tradition*. New York: Paulist, 1996.

D'Angelo, Mary Rose. "Images of Jesus and the Christian Call in the Gospels of Mark and Matthew." *Spirituality Today* 36 (1984): 220–36.

———. "Images of Jesus and the Christian Call in the Gospels of Luke and John." *Spirituality Today* 37 (1985): 196–212.

Danker, Frederick William, ed. *A Greek-English Lexicon of the New Testament and other Early Christian Literature*. 3rd ed. Chicago: The University of Chicago Press, 2000. Revised based on Walter Bauer's *Griechisch-deutsches Wörterbuch den Schriften des Neuen Testaments und der frühchristlichen Literatur*, 6th ed.; and on previous English editions by W. F. Arndt, F. W. Gingrich, and F. W. Danker.

Day, Dorothy. *The Long Loneliness: The Autobiography of Dorothy Day*. New York: Harper and Brothers, 1952.

Doohan, Helen. *Paul's Vision of Church*. Wilmington, DE: Glazier, 1989.

———. *Prayer in the New Testament: Make Your Requests Known to God*. Collegeville, MN: Liturgical Press, 1992.

Doohan, Leonard. *John: Gospel for a New Age*. Santa Fe: Bear and Co., 1988.

———. *Luke: The Perennial Spirituality*. Santa Fe: Bear and Co., 1985.

———. *Mark: Visionary of early Christianity*. Santa Fe: Bear and Co., 1986.

———. *Matthew: Spirituality for the 80s and 90s*. Santa Fe: Bear and Co., 1985.

———. "Scripture and Contemporary Spirituality." *Spirituality Today* 42 (1990): 62–74.

Downey, Michael. *Understanding Christian Spirituality*. New York: Paulist, 1997.

Eusebius. *The Ecclesiastical History*. Vol. II, 6.14.7. Translated by J. E. L. Oulton. Cambridge, MA: Harvard University Press, 1956.

Flannery, Austin, OP, ed. *Dei Verbum* (The Dogmatic Constitution on Divine Revelation). *Vatican Council II: Volume 1, The Conciliar and Post Conciliar Documents*. Northport, NY: Costello, 1996.

Gutierrez, Gustavo. *We Drink from Our Own Wells: The Spiritual Journey of a People*. Translated by Matthew J. O'Connell. Maryknoll, NY: Orbis Books, 1985.

Harrington, Daniel J., SJ. *The Gospel of Matthew*. Sacra Pagina Series. Vol. 1. Collegeville, MN: Liturgical Press, 1991.

Hartin, Patrick J. *A Spirituality of Perfection: Faith in Action in the Letter of James*. Collegeville, MN: Liturgical Press, 1999.

Holt, Bradley P. *Thirsty for God: A Brief History of Christian Spirituality*. 2nd ed. Minneapolis: Fortress, 2005.

Johnson, Elizabeth A. *She Who Is: The Mystery of God in Feminist Theological Discourse*. New York: Crossroad, 1992.

Johnson, Luke T. *Faith's Freedom: A Classic Spirituality for Contemporary Christians*. Minneapolis: Fortress/Augsburg, 1990.

Karris, Robert J. *Prayer and the New Testament: Jesus and His Communities at Worship*. New York: Crossroad, 2000.

Kloppenborg, John S. *Q, The Earliest Gospel: An Introduction to the Original Stories and Sayings of Jesus*. Louisville, KY: Westminster John Knox Press, 2008.

Koeppel, Josephine, OCD, trans. *Life in a Jewish Family: Her Unfinished Autobiographical Account*. The Collected Works of Edith Stein. Vol. 1. Washington, DC: ICS Publications, 1986.

———, trans. *Self-Portrait in Letters: 1916–1942*. The Collected Works of Edith Stein. Vol. 5. Washington, DC: ICS Publications, 1993.

Kugler, Robert, and Patrick Hartin. "Chapter 49: The Gospel of Mark." In *An Introduction to the Bible*. Grand Rapids, MI: William B. Eerdmans Publishing Company, 2009.

Malbon, Elizabeth Struthers. "Fallible Followers: Women and Men in the Gospel of Mark." *Semeia* 28 (1983): 29–48.

Martini, Carlo. *The Joy of the Gospel*. Collegeville, MN: Liturgical Press, 1994.

Metzger, Bruce M. "The Making of Ancient Books." Chap. 1 in *The Text of the New Testament: Its Transmission, Corruption and Restoration.* 2nd ed. Oxford: Clarendon Press, 1968.

———. *A Textual Commentary on the Greek New Testament.* Corrected ed. London/ New York: United Bible Societies, 1975.

Meyer, Robert T., trans. *St Athanasius: The Life of Saint Antony.* Ancient Christian Writers. Westminster, MD: The Newman Press, 1950.

Nouwen, Henri J. M. Foreword in *The Church Is All of You: Thoughts of Archbishop Oscar Romero,* translated by James R. Brockman. Minneapolis: Winston Press, 1984.

Oben, Freda Mary, trans. *Essays on Woman.* The Collected Works of Edith Stein. Vol. 2. Washington, DC: ICS Publications, 1987.

Pazdan, Mary Margaret. *Becoming God's Beloved in the Company of Friends: A Spirituality of the Fourth Gospel.* Eugene, OR: Cascade, 2007.

Quinn, John R. "The Relation of Moral Life and Moral Laws." *Origins* (May 30, 1996): 26–30.

Random House: Webster's College Dictionary. New York: Random House, 1995.

Ratzinger, Joseph (Pope Benedict XVI). *Jesus of Nazareth: From the Baptism in the Jordan to the Transfiguration.* New York: Doubleday, 2007.

Ricoeur, Paul. *Interpretation Theory: Discourse and the Surplus of Meaning.* Fort Worth, TX: Texas Christian University Press, 1976.

Roberts, Alexander, and James Donaldson, eds. "The Martyrdom of Perpetua and Felicitas." Appendix V. In *The Ante-Nicene Fathers: Translations of the Writings of the Fathers down to A.D. 325,* translated by R. E. Wallis, 697–706. Vol. III. New York: Charles Scribner's Sons, 1903.

Schneiders, Sandra M. "Biblical Spirituality." *Interpretation* 56, no. 2 (April 2002): 133–42.

———. *The Revelatory Text: Interpreting the New Testament as Sacred Scripture.* 2nd ed. Collegeville, MN: Liturgical Press, 1999.

———. "Theology and Spirituality: Strangers, Rivals, or Partners?" *Horizons* (Villanova) 13/2 (1986): 253–74.

Sheen, Fulton J. *Guide to Contentment.* Canfield, OH: Alba House, St Pauls, 1996.

Stevenson, Robert Louis. *Father Damien: An Open Letter to the Reverend Doctor Hyde of Honolulu from Robert Louis Stevenson.* London: Chatto and Windus, 1914.

Sullivan, John, OCD. *Edith Stein: Essential Writings.* Modern Spiritual Masters Series. Maryknoll, NY: Orbis Books, 2002.

Taylor, Charles. *Sources of the Self: The Making of the Modern Identity.* Cambridge, MA: Harvard University Press, 1989.

———. *Varieties of Religion Today: William James Revisited.* Cambridge, MA: Harvard University Press, 2002.

Williams, Rowan. *The Wound of Knowledge: Christian Spirituality from the New Testament to St John of the Cross.* 2nd ed. Boston, MA: Cowley Publications, 1990.

Wilson, Archbishop Philip. "Shaping the Future of the Church." *Origins* (May 2007): 37–41.

Index of Persons and Subjects